FROM ROMANCE TO RIOT
A SEATTLE MEMOIR

FROM ROMANCE TO RIOT
A SEATTLE MEMOIR
by Cal McCune

ISBN
0-9650248-0-6

Designed by Marie McCaffrey.
Cover photos by Alan Lande

I dedicate this book to Peg,
who for 63 years has tried to keep me out
of trouble.

Table of Contents

Introduction   3

1. The Long Ago: Drumaloor to Seattle   7

2. Wiseman's Makes Matrimony Possible   25

3. The Rolling Main and Beyond   39

4. Run Up the Storm Flag   59

5. University District Movement   73

6. Floyd the Flag Burner   83

7. The Sky Falls   91

8. We Play with Matches and High Explosives   101

9. University District Center: Birth, Life, and Death   109

10. Kent State: the Police Even the Score   117

11. The Mall: an Idea Whose Time Has Yet to Come   125

12. How Now Brown Cow   131

Appendix   140

In Appreciation

Priscilla Long: I thank her for her expertise in taming my verbal aberrations. I finally caught on that the period goes inside the quotation mark and that the possessive *its* has no apostrophe.

Marie McCaffrey: I thank her for the excellent design of this book.

Dean and Joy Worcester: I thank them for their constant encouragement and friendship.

I am grateful to my children, Leslie and Cal, Jr., and to Peg, for their loyal support. This memoir belongs not only to Seattle but to them.

Finally I shall in the future be forever grateful to those of you who now look at the low price and purchase this book.

Introduction

This book begins with my experiences as a small town boy born in 1911 in Polk, Nebraska. I was eight when my parents moved to Haxtun, Colorado and about then I also became fascinated with Seattle, and a girl named Peg. Our parents' relationship had begun in the Nebraska days and resulted in frequent visits on the part of our mothers back and forth between Haxtun and Seattle. Our fathers disliked each other. Mine thought Peg's a stuffy, high collar Republican and rejoiced when he was defeated for the United States Senate. Peg's had little in common with a table pounding Democrat.

Both had unrealized elements of greatness. Peg's father, an English immigrant, had clawed his way from being a penniless farm boy to membership on the Seattle City Council and later on the Superior Court Bench. His failings can be seen in the fact that he rose early every Sunday morning to destroy the comic section of the Seattle *Times*.

My father too lacked the common touch. Only his close friend Roy Chaney, the local liquor store proprietor whom Dad, a prohibitionist, tried to put out of business called him Calmar. Others called him Mr. McCune. Dad wondered "Why?"

I concluded it was because my father neither told dirty stories nor swore. I busied myself learning to do both. This effort ended abruptly when I was about fifteen. I had a temporary job in a car repair establishment and was standing in the pit under a Willys-Knight trying to pull the cylinder sleeves. What better opportunity to demonstrate my new vocabulary. If the Devil was listening he must have chuckled. As it turned out the shop suddenly went quiet. Curious, I peered out

Cal and Peg McCune on their voyage to Victoria and marriage.

3

under the running board. My father was looking down with tears running down his cheeks. He turned and walked away. Niether of us ever mentioned the incident.

I first enrolled at the University of Washington in 1930 but dropped in and out of school until I moved to Seattle in the fall of 1931. Two years later Peg and I were married.

My memoir concludes soon after the debacle at Kent State in May, 1970 when Ohio National Guardsmen fired into an antiwar demonstration killing four students. In Seattle I spent part of the night in my darkened law office with my Dad's old double barreled shotgun resting on the arms of the chair. I was destined to be arrested that same night for interfering with the police.

In between I attended the University of Washington and presided over the double sink at Wiseman's Cafe, an establishment noted in the 1930's as a sobering up pitstop on the way home from the speak-easy. During the 1940's Peg and I lived with our two children on the Anna Lou, a tubby forty footer, known in Seattle as a Dream Boat. Ours was the only vessel moored at the Seattle Yacht Club that ever sported (instead of a pennant) an Opening Day sign reading "QUARANTINE - MUMPS."

More than anything else these recollections center on the 1960's. They depict a frightened and perplexed University and business community as viewed by a University District lawyer who put his reputation on the line, lost part of it, and had the time of what otherwise would have been a prosaic middle-aged life. It was a time of drugs, riots, marches, bombs, and flag burning. Litigating over disputed property lines was never so much fun.

I have now practiced law behind the same desk in the University District for 50 years. If my luck holds, I hope to drop dead at that desk but not before the year 2000. The desk contains little that relates to this book except memories and an envelope full of marijuana leaves.

This is not only my story but Seattle's story. I like to think that it has some elements of an epic account reflecting the eternal struggle of men and women to overcome their personal destiny, to serve a cause, or to tear society asunder.

Chapter 1

The Long Ago: Drumaloor to Seattle

W hen the McCune clan gathered at Thanksgiving in Stromsburg, Nebraska it was Grandmother who carved the turkey and asked, pointing at the tail, "Who wants the Pope's nose?" Not an unusual comment for a Scotch-Irish emigrant born and raised in County Cavan in Northern Ireland. Her people were Protestants lured or transported to Northern Ireland by the British Crown anxious to counter the troublesome Catholics who wanted their own freedom.

Uncle Wesley's first automobile in 1903 had a steering lever. This group includes Grandmother McCune, Uncle Wesley, Aunt Margaret, and their son Jim Wilson.

I have often wondered how she would have reacted when her son, my father, sided with the local Catholics against the Ku Klux Klan.

County Cavan where Grandmother was born and raised abuts Protestant-dominated Ulster. In Grandmother's day neither Catholics nor Protestants dominated County Cavan. No surprise then that Grandmother took part in the rivalry between the two religions.

The potato famine of 1841-1851 resulted in some million deaths and prompted both Catholics and Protestants to think of emigrating. An equal number did so, primarily to the United States. Grandmother was a child during the famine. As a young woman in the 1860's she was brought to the United States by her brother James Bell who had emigrated a few years earlier. The only reminder that they once lived in County Cavan is the huge granite tombstone that James erected over his mother's grave. It stands in a lonely overgrown cemetery on the Drumaloor Road near a crumbling stone building.

Of their father the family records tell little. There is a daguerreotype that shows Charles Bell looking stern and quite Puritanical. We know he was a landowner with a substantial house

Great Grandfather Charles Bell and Great Grandmother Margaret Bell, taken from daguereotypes made about 1860.

and outbuildings. When I visited Drumaloor in 1953 I saw them in ruins. I brought home a piece of slate from the broken down roof. When my grandmother died in 1922, communication with the past was cut off. Like so many of the young, I had never sought her story while she lived.

Grandmother was a true matriarch. She presided over what we would call today an extended family with a determination that included, almost incidentally, my rather frail grandfather. Calmar McCune was a semi-disabled Civil War veteran whom I remember lying in a hammock reading Dickens. Ours was a kissing type family and Grandfather's tobacco stained mustache left much to be desired. His faithful daughters, my aunts, attributed his use of chewing tobacco to the fact that it eased the pain of his disability— something about his innards that prevented his standing up except for short periods. Once, he told me, he went to hear a lecture by Booker T. Washington. The seats were taken and before he realized it he had stood for two hours listening in fascination.

My father's sisters, Eva and Daisy, often bragged to their children about how Grandfather was the Stromsburg, Nebraska Temperance Mayor. When I was fourteen my father confided that until he was ten his father had hit the bottle in the best Irish tradition. I promptly imparted this information to my cousins not realizing that it would cause my aunts to blow up like miniature Krakatoas.

My grandparents started their married life in 1873 by homesteading in a sod house near Osceola, Nebraska. It was there my father was born. There were no fences and except for going around the low hills, everyone traveled on horseback by the straightest route. They raised chickens and vegetables, owned two horses and a cow. Game was plentiful — grouse, prairie chickens, ducks, geese, and an occasional antelope. The buffalo were no more but their chips remained to be used in lieu of firewood.

Grandfather was often gone. Sometimes he would be working in near-by Osceola but at other times, I suspect, he would be indulging his favorite pastime. Because Grandmother was fearful of the Indians who often showed up at the door, they moved first into Osceola and later to Stromsburg. Grandfather tried many vocations, from editing a Democratic newspaper in a Republican county to managing one of his brothers-in-law James Bell's grain elevators. He worked earnestly but not well. While running the elevator he wrote all checks for grain in dollar amounts, making up the difference out of petty cash. James Bell's bookkeeper had fits but Grandpa wouldn't change.

James Bell, tall and dignified with a plume of white hair and a mustache, turned out to be a Horatio Alger. He built one of the first power plants in Nebraska and controlled a string of grain elevators. I am sure he helped my grandparents acquire the acreage that for almost thirty years was to be a Kingdom presided over by my grandmother.

James preferred being around his sister, my grandmother, more than his wife. He enlarged the McCune house to accommodate his presence. According to my father, he lived there on weekends and often during the week sans spouse until his death in 1912.

The next arrival to my grandmother's household was John Wesley Wilson, a wealthy Swedish landowner and businessman who wore a gold chain across his vest and who dined with his own huge napkin tucked under his chin. For many years he had worshipped from afar my aunt Margaret, the oldest daughter. They were finally married in 1899. Everyone agreed that, with her interest in music, thoughtfulness, and happy disposition, she was a rare person. Again the house was remodeled and extended. Their son James Wilson, of whom more later, was born there in 1900.

With Grandmother calling the shots, this human anthill with its immense lawn, tennis court, a St. Bernard named Watch, and Uncle

Wesley's huge 1907 Winton Six automobile lasted until 16 January 1916 when Margaret, always frail, died of flu and pneumonia at the age of forty-three.

I doubt if Grandmother's world could be duplicated even in today's Camelots of the rich. Today entertainment is purchased, the comings and goings often have a political thrust. The family frequents the salons of London and Paris with the homestead Camelot becoming a mere way point on life's adventures. In Stromsburg entertainment was home grown. It involved, one must admit, the upper echelons of the community. It was an island of plenty, and the sea of misery surrounding it was accepted as normal. Destitution and early mortality were a given.

Lest one forget, not until 1929 did the practice end of loading orphans, girls and boys in the crowded cities of the East onto trains. They were then sent West to be arbitrarily selected by settlers. Many found loving homes, but for others it was a sentence to hard labor. Children not chosen faced an uncertain future at the end of the line.

Her offspring maintained in later years that Grandmother ruled with love, not an iron rod. There were no arguments, rather a unique amalgam of love and affection. Life in Stromsburg swirled around the estate. There were social events, musicals, readings, and discussion. Dad played cornet in the town band and helped hunt the passenger pigeon to extinction. He owned a long coat lined with buffalo hide that after his death I treasured until it fell apart.

In 1907 my father and two of his brothers-in-law founded the town of Polk thirteen muddy miles from Stromsburg. My father became a small town banker. He and his Partners had confidence in the permanence of the horse and buggy and of the railroad. Towns appeared every few miles along the railroads to supply all the essentials a farming community might need.

Also in 1907, my father married Grace Montgomery, a visiting York, Nebraska girl whom he met on the family tennis court. In Polk my parents built a large house with a garden and tennis court. I was born in the north bedroom. In the den I often lay on the St. Bernard, Watch, who by then had died and served as a rug on the floor.

I had the run of the town and I was probably regarded as more blight than blessing. I suspect I had a nasty disposition. This was borne out years later. When we moved to Haxtun, Colorado, several of Dad's friends came along. One of them, Freeman Hahn, made it clear he wanted nothing to do with me. I finally asked my father why?

"Son, when you were about four you fell down on the sidewalk. Mr Hahn picked you up. You kicked him in the shin and said 'God damn you.'"

Once, before the new Methodist church was built, the preacher's daughter and I quite innocently used the mens' three holer outhouse behind the church at the same time. My mother was out hanging washlaundry and spotted us. It was one of the rare occasions when the stick was brought to bear.

Mrs. Tenney, a stooped-over old lady who always wore black, had no love for me or my dog Teddy, a white fox terrier with an uncertain disposition. She claimed that I commanded Teddy to "sic em," which I didn't, but it is true that Teddy shredded the hem of her long black dress. For two months Teddy and I were required to pay her weekly visits. Each week I would apologize and tell her how virtuous Teddy had become. This was not entirely accurate. I am sure it was Teddy who broke into the pen and killed six of her chickens.

Finally Dad could put up no longer with Teddy's zest for living dangerously. I was out walking with my mother when I saw the town handyman driving by with Teddy in the front seat.

"There's Teddy!" I shouted.

"The nice man's taking him for a ride," my mother explained.

That evening I searched the neighborhood, whistling and looking for Teddy. Finally Dad caught up with me, put has hand on my shoulder and assured me that Teddy would be all right. He had gone to live with another family where he would be happier. I don't recall, but I probably cried a bit after going to bed, clutching a piece of silk I loved to hold at night.

The next day a new Teddy arrived, another white fox terrier with brown spots. For years this Teddy spent much of his time beside my father's desk. He also loved to hunt ground squirrels. Years later after my mother died, Teddy searched for her for months sniffing embarrassingly at any woman wearing a fur collar.

My most vivid memory of Polk is the night they later called the "false armistice." As I recall it was the night before the real armistice on 11 November 1918, the end of World War I. Dad got me out of bed and we walked hand in hand toward a din of shots, shouts, and explosions in the center of town. In front of the hotel, rifles were popping away at a stuffed Kaiser strung from the power line. Down an alley the town blacksmith, Herman Brown, squat and sturdy, was setting off what I assume were nitro-glycerine caps between a sledge hammer and an anvil.

We moved to Haxtun, Colorado in the spring of 1919. There my father again went into business as a banker, with disastrous results.

I had always thought we moved to Haxtun because my mother disliked the hot summer nights and wished to live near her brother and sister. There was a more important factor.

When my parents built their home in Haxtun it had a large recreation room. In it my Dad installed a billiard table, a ping pong table, boxing gloves, a punching bag, a small pool table, and a huge wrestling mat that when not in use hung against the wall on block and tackle. Dad never used any of it but made it known that one night a week it was open to any young people who might wish to enjoy it. Many did.

Years later Dad and I visited Polk including the church he and my mother had helped finance. The door was open and we had entered the basement when the minister showed up with a "what's your mission brother?" approach. I was to learn from my father the history of our recreation room.

Dad and my mother had helped finance the church with the understanding that at least a portion of the basement could be used by the town's young people and that the church would acquire the equipment my father specified.

All went well until opening day when a rumble of discontent became a cyclone and Dad's plans were blown away. Certain members of the congregation would not tolerate what they considered evil activity in the basement of the church.

Perhaps my father and mother had been too optimistic. In any event they bought the equipment and took it West in a box car.

I have it on good authority that until recently, at least, you could hold a "Sing-Sing" in the church but not a dance. Goodbye Polk. Hello Haxtun.

Haxtun was and still is a tiny oasis in the semi-arid, dusty and windblown northeastern Colorado plain. Today the businesses I knew are gone from its main street and the Haxtun Bulldogs, once a powerhouse, play football in a league with eight players on a side. The whistle is silent that once blew at six to make sure we were preparing for work. The town's whistle has become a siren that screams at 7:00 a.m., again at noon, at 1:00 p.m. and finally at 6:00 p.m. It no longer sounds at 8:45 to announce that all good boys and girls should be at home. In the old days when the 8:45 whistle blew we were likely to be out tramping through the neighbors' gardens playing run-sheep-run. The steam (later diesel) power plant is silent. Now the thump of its diesel engine can be heard only when the Rural Electrification Authority supply breaks down. An acerbic old German, John Kirchoffer, ran the power plant with its immense open switches that would give fits to today's safety inspectors. When I was a boy we developed a rather strained friendship with my visits usually ending with "now get the hell out of here."

I would go home and tinker in my tiny shop. Mostly I played with electricity, a carbon arc and a hydrogen generator, building crystal radio sets that didn't work even after hours of tuning. Later I built vacuum tube sets that did work. It was a triumph when I could call Dad to listen to the faint call letters of KDKA in Pittsburgh. On one occasion the Model T spark coil I was experimenting with somehow joined forces with the telephone line and severely hampered service to the customers of Mr. Brook's Haxtun Telephone Company.

The Haxtun I knew changed in a number of ways. In the late 1930's and 1940's a few increasingly wealthy farmers began buying up the original 160 acre homesteads. Houses and barns were torn down and the size of a family farm increased to perhaps 1600 acres. Automobiles provided easy access to nearby centers such as Sterling. My father had once delighted in taking me and my contemporaries to Denver. In 1926 many of them had never seen the white capped Rockies that rose majestically less than 180 miles away from Haxtun.

Most of Haxtun's business enterprises were doomed. But Haxtun today is no pocket of poverty. It has a delightful park, an excellent school system, huge grain elevators, and a sense of compassion. A few years ago I sent 300 dollars to the high school Principal to be given to a needy student. He wrote to the effect that they already had enough scholarships to go around but fortunately had found a student who wished to attend a beauty school in Sterling and had given her the 300 dollars. I never received a response from the recipient.

I would not recommend Haxtun to a free thinker. It is, as far as I can tell, almost overpoweringly Republican. Its most attended churches specialize in "hellfire and damnation." If Dad were alive today, I can't imagine him finding anyone with sufficient doubt to even argue about whether or not baptism was required to get the pearly gates to open.

I enjoyed reading. Besides the trash of my day such as Captain Billy's Whiz Bang, I reveled in the travels of Richard Haliburton and in the short stories of O. Henry. I became an agnostic thanks to Henrik VanLoon and Will Durant who spread the world's great religions and philosophies before me, making the summertime Methodist catechism seem puny by comparison. Tom Sawyer and Huck Finn were forbidden and of course widely read.

Growing up I developed a great love for my father. He built a mammoth box-kite that we flew together, and he read to me when I was sick. He taught me to hunt. Above all he forgave my faults and understood my failures. To this day my decision making often involves the question of what my father would have done.

My mother died in 1925 when I was 14. It was very painful and I pretty much blocked out her memory. It all came back when I began to write this. She made certain I had a set of Montessori inserts and could fit them quickly into the spaces provided. She made delicacies such as a white custard full of nuts to encourage me to eat when I was sick. She taught me to make fudge and taffy. Above all she bought me books and magazines.

She died on 22 February 1925 of erysipelas, a disease that itself has now fallen victim to antibiotics. It began with a red blotch that could spread and kill. Dr. McKnight fought it with an ever expanding back-fire of silver nitrate. It was not a new ordeal for my mother. Her once beautiful face was already scarred from previous attacks. For almost a week, conversations were whispered as her condition worsened. Death stalking a victim was something I had never experienced. I didn't cry until, on the final day, I wandered down to the basement. My father was in the recreation room kneeling with his hands on the edge of the billiard table. With an agony I never heard again he was pleading for the life of my mother.

"Please, God, don't take her away."

Stumbling to my bedroom, I cried while making a firm resolve that if his prayer remained unanswered I myself would never pray again. I now do so only as a perfunctory gesture to others. When I was once asked to give the benediction at my Rotary Club I agreed but said I would recite Matthew Arnold's "Dover Beach." I was never asked again.

Early that afternoon our huge Edison phonograph was moved into the bedroom near my mother and the sounds of a Strauss waltz echoed in the silent house. I cornered Doc McKnight.

"Is she going to die?".

"Yes son. She's dying now."

The town said farewell to her with a massive turnout but I simply didn't listen to the funeral. Later we rode to the Sedgwick Depot in Del Banister's air cooled Franklin automobile following the tail light of the hearse as it bounced over the frozen gravel road. My mother was to be buried in Nebraska. The night was cold and clear and the stars twinkled like diamonds. Sedgwick was a flag stop: the train crew was in a hurry. Dad and I stood on the platform while the iron rimmed baggage wagon clattered to the hearse and the casket was transferred to the train.

A hearse and a car driven by one of Dad's friends were waiting at Grand Island, Nebraska. There was a brief graveside ceremony in Stromsburg and the next night Del Banister picked us up in a snow storm for a new beginning. I sometimes think of my mother alone in Stromsburg and wish I could spirit my father's casket there to lie beside her. I never heard him sing in his garden again.

That was the worst time but not the only bad time. One summer I was in old man Sam Winebar's dugout when, with a roar like a thousand trains, hail pelted the galvanized roof. It would have been his first wheat crop in four years. We had just pulled in with a combine to harvest it. Hail, drought, and grasshoppers had taken the others. In two days it would have been harvested.

As the hail died down he said blankly "It's gone." He lay down with his face to the concrete wall and sobbed. We suggested he go to town. He turned his face toward us. It was stubbled, red, and covered with tear-smeared dirt. "There's no place to go." He died soon after, never knowing that his farm lay astride the then unknown Ogallala Aquifer that would enrich his successors.

The 1920's were not kind to farmers or to their communities.

Around 1929 my father, after a long struggle, finally went, to use a colloquialism, flat ass broke. This was the first but not the last time. In 1926, the year after my mother died, he had to sell our house, which became a hospital. My young brother was sent to live temporarily with relatives in Denver. Dad rented two rooms. We slept together, and boarded with Mrs. Brooks.

In 1929 Dad, still President of the bank, had made improvident personal investments in German Marks, which soon turned into bales of paper, and in a failed hog ranch. He'd also made some bad loans to farmers on behalf of the bank. His shirt if not lost was badly tattered. In part what follows reflects his desperate efforts in the late 20's and early 30's to recoup his fortunes.

Perhaps because almost everyone was equally impoverished it was not a bad life. There was much to do on nickels and dimes including Saturday night at the Rialto, a long, narrow, 1915 version of a movie theater. A piano, with bursts of fury, followed the exploits of the silent film star Tom Mix with his white sombrero, who always found a way to save the girl. When the film broke and the projector flooded the screen with intense white light, tiny white patches would show up. The source was not difficult to find. If you sat close to the screen during the show, you could often hear the snap and plop of a slingshot sending a staple through the screen.

My buddy, Buster Meakins, and I hunted, fished, and frolicked with the girls in a rather restrained way. In our freshman year a fellow classmate caught the "clap." We worried about his recovery in whispered conversations. For a while at least, our class became a virgin generation.

Dad began to make a modest financial come-back. He rented a house and my brother Wes came home at last.

Looking back, as writing this book has required, I for the first time realized what a disappointment I must have been to my father. Consider my musical career. My mother had insisted that I learn to play the piano. Commencing when I was nine, I made weekly pilgrimages to Mae Becker's home. I am sure Mrs. Becker soon realized that I was tone deaf and had a weird approach to keeping time. My mother kept her hopes up and I did a daily stint at the piano, eventually learning to play "Let Me Call You Sweetheart," and "Always." After Bus Meakins and I became pals I had a wild dream that with

Bus playing his saxophone and me the piano we could supplant Virginia Carlson who played piano during the silent films at the Rialto. Bus was bright enough to realize my shortcomings.

Dad urged me to play his cornet and described the joys of playing in the town band. I took a "why not you" attitude. He finally hit on the answer by buying a bass horn. No worry about developing a firm lip. Just learn the fingering and blow into it at appropriate times. This turned out to be the problem.

For three Saturday nights I played in the town band on the veranda of the Legion Hall basking in the adulation of the occupants of several dozen cars parked in front and blocking the street. Then it ended. X. A. Lambert, the Band's indispensable star cornetist, in front of God and everybody, as we used to say, issued a proclamation. "Get that McCune kid out of here or I'm quitting the band."

I replaced music with my Dad's ancient model T truck. My cousin, Cal Reedy, had come from Denver and we planned to make our fortune hauling grain from farmers' fields to the grain elevator. It might have worked except that we no sooner made a few dollars than a tire would blow out. We netted nine dollars for the summer. In any event Cal took my place in the band. When it came time to play the County Fair we drove the 21 miles to Holyoke in my "strip" model T. I had removed the exhaust manifold. It made a heck of a racket and a sheet of blue flame at night. I don't remember the Fair, just roaring down the road with the high pitched scream of the exhaust and Cal in the other jump seat blasting away at the sky on the bass horn. Must have made the farmers wonder what was happening to the Nation's youth.

Dad had acquired a Twin City tractor. During the summer I was 15, Buster and I took turns mounting the tractor and pulling a one-way plow four hours on and four off. "Off" during the day meant sleeping under the truck bed and devouring pulp magazines. At night a string from the operator's wrist to the throttle provided hope that if the driver dozed and fell off, the engine would kill before he went under the plow. The North Platte airway beacon 100 miles away reassuringly swept the horizon, but the tumble weeds the wind blew out of the darkness into our spotlight beam always startled me as my mind translated them into monsters. We weren't exactly dedicated to our work and looked forward to the rare rain shower or Saturday night when we could head for Haxtun and perhaps blow ourselves to a banana split at Monty's Drug. I doubt that Dad, whose mechanical ability never progressed beyond driving nails, realized how much danger we were courting.

It was my father who pushed me into the educational process. Probably he remembered his own dreams shattered by the depression of 1893.

The year 1928-29 was a glorious one. Farming was in my blood. Buster and I attended Colorado Aggies. Free of parental restraint we went all out to live the collegiate life. Typical was the wintery day we loaded two girls in my Model A roadster and set off for a football game in Denver. Half way through the game it began snowing heavily. When the game ended we knew we were in trouble. We put the girls on the special train to Fort Collins.

"Let's meet the train," Bus suggested. Why not? With one of us manning the hand operated windshield swipes we took off. We came close to killing ourselves when we spun out of control descending a hill outside Loveland. We arrived in Ft. Collins in time to see the last passengers leaving the train. Our dates, we found later, had gone home with more reliable escorts; perhaps seniors?

I was 17 and Dad had entrusted me with a checkbook. I never balanced it and apparently Dad didn't either.

I remember him sitting at his desk in the almost defunct bank. He looked old and tired. I thought he might cry.

"Son, how in God's name did you manage to spend 930 dollars?"

I waffled around about the cost of higher education but I'm sure that he correctly concluded that I had flung most of it away. It was the last year I attended a football game.

In 1930 going to the University of Nebraska was an easy decision. I could room with my cousin, Cal Ready. In addition, while on a Christmas visit to Dad's sister in Lincoln, Jim Wilson, my Stromsburg cousin, had arranged a blind date for me to attend a dance at the Cornhusker. My date was a Junior and I can vividly remember her doing the Charleston. Unfortunately by the time I arrived at the University she had left and I was left only with the problem of how to survive.

Survival took many turns. I lasted one long day at a Piggly Wiggly grocery and was paid two dollars. At midnight the manager finally asked me what I did at the bank for which I claimed to have worked. I had to confess that I had been the janitor.

Next, I delivered handbills door to door and also handed them out across from the Campus. I had been ogling a cute blonde who wore a fur coat. She was in my Spanish class and obviously out of my class as well. All hope was lost when I handed her a handbill.

Finally I hit on selling Fuller Brushes door to door. Except for attending weekly evening sessions at which we sang stupid songs about the company, I found it enjoyable. The free scrub brush housewives were accustomed to receiving opened almost any door and I could spread out my wares on the floor. They ranged from an assortment of brushes to perfumed bath soap. At least a small sale was almost certain. The only problem was that before long the delivery of purchases took up almost as much time as selling.

I might have continued at the University except for an unfortunate incident on the Crete road at 3:00 a.m., as recounted in embarrassing detail on the front page of the Nebraska State Journal to which unfortunately my father subscribed. My Model T roadster hit a frozen block of dirt and rolled over twice. We all, including the girl on my lap, my cousin who was driving, and his date, exited where the top had been. No serious injuries except my date who spent two nights in the hospital and my own fractured ankle. At the end of the semester I drove what was left of my windshieldless Ford 300 miles back to Haxtun in a blizzard.

By this time Dad again had been financially derailed. He personally had guaranteed the paper of Jack Hartman, a friend who was the local John Deere implement dealer. When Jack abandoned the business Dad took it over in desperation. We labored in the damn business for months. I went to John Deere tractor school and held myself forth as an expert tractor repairman. We composed a letter to John Deere begging for a job for Dad. No luck. They finally shut us down and Dad went into bankruptcy. Eventually he paid off all his creditors with the exception of John Deere. They deserved the loss.

What next? As I've explained, my mother had frequently taken my brother and me to Seattle where she visited her friend from their days in York, Nebraska. On our visits I learned to love the forests and lakes, and Seattle's seven hills. I must confess that I even savored the haze and the odor of wood burning in mills and forests. Our mothers once took Peg and me for a glorious month on the beach at Copalis, Washington. It was there while fishing, crabbing, and clam digging that we cemented our relationship.

Peg several times had visited Haxtun with her mother. During those visits I taught Peg how to shoot rabbits. In retrospect I realize she was a bit squeamish. We wandered among the willows in the dry bed of Sand Creek where I sought to gain her approval by throwing rocks at the snakes in the pools.

After Peg's visit I would write her postcards which I never sent. Probably they were concerned with important matters such as how many fish I had caught at the Sedgwick Reservoir. Years later I found that Dad had bundled them up and sent them.

In 1931 a friend, Loren "Andy" Anderson, a recent high school graduate, and I headed west in another 25 dollars Model T. We arrived in Seattle almost penniless. Andy, who was more personable, soon got a job waiting table at the University Commons.

It was to be a great year. Dad, who was selling insurance and managing farms, occasionally managed to tuck ten dollars into one of his letters. I bought a set of stencils and paint and talked housewives into paying fifty cents to have house numbers painted on the curb. In those days they would open their doors. Andy and I lodged in a basement room in return for which we did yard work. I worked evenings in a delicatessen for dinner plus five dollars a week. We both had paper routes. I also got a job at the Commons on campus. However, on my first night waiting banquet tables, I dropped a tray of pie ala mode. It was only the ice cream that fell on the floor. When Miss Terry spotted me putting it back on the pie, my career on campus ended abruptly.

That summer it was back to the tractor and in the fall I hitch-hiked to Seattle where I continued my love affair with Peg. But by the end of winter quarter I was broke and desperate.

At that point a letter arrived from my cousin, Jim Wilson. Jim had developed a lecture series by recounting with slides a motorcycle trip he had taken across the Sahara. Jim suggested I come to Indiana and help book lecture dates. I hitchhiked to Chicago and on to the home of Jim and Alice Wilson in the Indiana dunes. It turned out that Jim could lecture better than I could sell. I drove Jim's old Chevrolet through Indiana and Illinois. At night I slept in the car beside secluded roads. I rose at dawn, put on Jim's spare suit, drank a bottle of milk and drove into a nearby city to find the program chairman of the local Rotary Club, a post that in future years I myself would hold.

On my 21st birthday I sold a lecture in LaFayette, Indiana. In celebration of both events I decided to go to an early show. After the show I got in the car and drove off. At the first corner, a rear axle broke. The wheel didn't come off. A nearby garage with an attendant on duty provided a solution. I had four dollars. For two dollars they would let me work at the shop until eight a.m. At dawn I could walk to a junk yard and buy an axle. It all worked out with a quarter to spare. Small solace to find that for three dollars and 75 cents the garage would have done the job.

My bookings were meager and after three months we mutually agreed I was an impediment and should hitchhike back to Colorado.

Dad remarried in 1933. I had already left home except for going back to help with the harvest during my vacations, the last time in 1945. But I soon began to feel that both Wes and I had acquired a new mother. She was Ellen Bentson. Born in a sod house north of Haxtun, she loved us both and our children learned to worship her.

Her Swedish frugality was sharpened by the frontier. Dust, locusts, hail, and 100 mile trips by buggy in order to room in Greeley and take business courses spelled out her drive for success. Ellen had worked as a teller in Dad's bank until it closed. After their marriage they jointly operated an insurance and real estate office in the building adjoining the old bank which had become the Town Hall. When the bank was still operating with her in the teller's cage, I vividly recall her startled look when I slipped on the ice and fell through the plate glass of the front door.

She was stubborn. It was her practice when running water in the kitchen sink to fill a watering can until the hot water arrived. She would then pour this water on the garden. On one occasion it was raining. My father suggested that it was a waste of effort to water the garden. With tears in her eyes Ellen stood in the rain and dumped her contribution. I wasn't proud of my father and wished he would take her in his arms. Ellen survived my father and died of a heart attack almost 25 years ago. She was a gallant woman.

An uncle who was Assistant State Highway Engineer for Colorado bailed me out in 1932 by finagling a job on a road crew. The foreman made a point of telling everyone how I had gotten my 50 cent an hour job. The several bullies on the crew made the first month pure hell.

The gravel was not up to grade and it was necessary for someone, guess who, to stand beside a conveyor belt lifting chunks of granite from a pile and putting them on the belt. My shift was 4.00 a.m. until noon. By seven I was in the final throes of dying. Shorty, the foreman, would come by at frequent intervals to see if I was dead. In between his visits I would swig from the water jug. When he came by I would throw up. Surely he would not want to kill my uncle's darling. Finally I found the solution. It delayed my demise for a couple of days until I toughened up. Quite by accident, I discovered that if I put three huge pieces on the belt in rapid succession the crusher would plug up. The operator would have to climb up and dislodge my handiwork with a long iron bar. The gravel trucks would idle in an increasingly long line. Shorty would stand there looking up at the operator and cursing. I would dutifully watch the proceedings, leaning against the conveyor and laughing to myself. Had Shorty caught on I probably would have ended up on the conveyor belt.

The work completed near Fort Collins, the operation moved to Vona, Colorado, a tiny town that seemed to hover on the windy plain between life and death.

At Vona things simmered down when, in desperation and with a "whose next" attitude, I gently prodded a bully with a fork. He'd made it a point to sit next to me in the chuck wagon, using his obesity to push me down the bench. After that I sensed that I was no longer the low man on the totem pole and ate in peace except for the flies. On an unusually hot day they would drop on the table along with the goo from the fly catching strips hanging over head. Watch where you park the spuds!

One event stands out. Thanks to my uncle I was on a road that adjoined the Rock Island's main line, flagging truck drivers to direct them where to dump their loads of gravel. It was early in the morning, in September 1932. The sun was preparing to scorch the Colorado plain. Far down the track a west bound passenger train blew its whistle. In minutes it had roared past, but it left a message for a 21 year old lonely kid.

"The world was mine come hell or high water!" It was F.D.R.'s campaign special.

Chapter 2

Wiseman's Makes Matrimony Possible

I returned to Seattle in the fall of 1932 with just enough money, thanks to my highway engineer uncle, to enter law school. During most of law school I carried two jobs. Essential to my survival was the grave yard shift at Wiseman's.

Except for its macho orientation, Wiseman's would qualify for a modern sitcom. It was one of the few sobering up establishments in Seattle. The red neon coffee cup and it's sign, "Coffee That Brings You Back," told it all. Wiseman's was located in the University District in a converted house, just north of the University Book Store. From the alley today it looks much the same as it probably did almost 100 years ago.

At one end of the long serving bar Dick Wiseman presided over the cigar counter and cash register. At the other end I presided over a double sink. In between the stools were occupied by a night-long parade of customers. Some were philosophers, others drunks. A few were women and many were former football players lured by the prospect of pointing out their photograph on the wall. I disliked them because more than other customers they threw up in the can. "McCune, you'd better get the mop."

I did feel sorry for one. A big, blustery, half drunk guy, already turning to fat and baldness. "Hey fellows, wanna see my picture?

"Shit! It's gone. Hey Dick!"

"Sorry, got to make room for the new guys."

The room was long and narrow. It was dominated by Dick whose high pitched voice carried its length. The rattle of dice in the leather

University Way, including Wiseman's Cafe, in the 1930's. Photo Courtesy of Special Collections and Preservation Division, University of Washington Libraries.

cup as he played "double or nothing" with customers also carried far down the counter. Frequently a steady customer would come around my end of the counter and enter the back room. You could hear the whir and clatter of the illegal slots and occasionally, a rush of coins.

Dick had long, nicotine stained fingers, a sallow complexion befitting his night-owl lifestyle, and a narrow face. I neither liked nor disliked him but I liked him better when, years later, his widow told me what thin financial ice he had been skating on.

Dick's brother Burt was the day manager. I hardly knew him. I only remember that for a few months after prohibition was abolished and until someone looked up the law and found that Wiseman's was too close to the University, we sold beer. Dick experimented with various condiments before finally settling for pretzels. The customers particularly liked a small bone-shaped cookie that we served until Burt looked for his box of dog biscuits the label of which was turned toward the wall.

The Health Department made few if any inspections. Had they done so they would have found more than dog biscuits in the back room.

"What the hell is that smell?" Dick asked. He pointed at me because I mopped the floor.

I sniffed around ineffectively. A day or two later I was removing the day's supply of dill pickles from near the bottom of what must have been a fifty gallon dill pickle barrel. Only then did I find the dead rat. I can't recall whether or not we used the remaining pickles.

I regret that I learned so little about the restaurant business at Wiseman's. When not at the sink or wielding the mop I did learn to be a rather clumsy waiter but my cooking capabilities were limited to making our soap out of lye and fat skimmed off the soup kettle. Oh yes, I steamed and skinned the potatoes.

Two officers in a patrol car usually favored us with their patronage in the early hours. Under strict instructions their bills were reduced by one-half. After carefully selecting toothpicks they would walk out, while the slots clicked away in the back room and while Dick or Percy, who was a combination hanger-on and employee, rolled dice against meal tickets at the front counter and ran illegal punch boards that paid off in merchandise if you punched out the lucky number.

Dick usually went home around two or three in the morning and

Percy took over. I admired Percy. In spite of looking like a broken down prize fighter with his bulldog face, smashed nose, and fog horn voice with a raspy New York accent, Percy possessed dignity. He probably thought of me as the underling I was. For a few hours he was captain of the ship. He ran it well.

One of my duties was to get rid of passed out drunks. We had our own technique. Hold an ice-cube against the tendons and arteries on the under side of the wrist. In a minute the drunk would begin to stir. In another he was hurting like hell and trying to free himself from the ice cube. Before long he was awake and desperate. At that point two of us would strong-arm him out into the night and head him down the street.

Wiseman's was indifferent toward women. A few I remember vividly.

There was the nearly toothless, sloppily drunk old woman who wandered in early in the morning. "Where's your toilet?" she demanded.

"Ain't got one for women," Percy growled.

"The hell you don't." She barged into what was tastefully designated a "Wash Room." This was followed by a clatter of doors. A regular patron emerged, pulling up his pants. "My God! There's a woman in there."

In a minute she left, spitting on the floor as she passed the, for once, silent Percy.

There were other women of course. Those I remember sat opposite my double sink. The manager of the Coon Chicken Inn often showed up with a woman friend after that establishment near Lake City closed down at one o'clock. She was older than me and always made a number of suggestions about what we could do together. If my head got too close to the counter she would run a casual finger through my curly hair. Nothing came of our affair.

Far more interesting were Mike Foster and his wife Pam. Mike was a reporter on the Seattle *Post-Intelligencer* and they often came in together after the morning edition had been put to bed. Usually they had stopped for refreshments elsewhere en route. By the time they hit Wiseman's, Mike was pretty well sloshed. The thrust of his blustery comments to anyone in the vicinity was that he was the best and most unappreciated reporter on the P.I. He'd show them "by God," just wait until the book was finished. Pam, stone sober, would nod in agreement. I felt sorry for her and also thought her the prettiest woman who ever came into Wiseman's.

When I saw them for the last time Mike was beaming, and Pam looked happy. Mike had sold his book, *American Dream.*

"I did it!. I did it tonight!" Mike boasted somewhat groggily, "I told the son-of-a-bitch I quit!" Later I read his book with pleasure but I never saw either of them again. I feel I witnessed the opening scene of "An American Tragedy."

A few years after I left in 1934, Wiseman's lost its lease and moved to the 4200 block of University Way. Dick sold the business and retired. A few years later Dick died. I am sure my probate fee for handling his substantial estate exceeded any sum he had paid me as a dishwasher. Wiseman's lingered until the 1960's and will next appear in these chronicles on the night of the bombing.

I have had a sixty year love affair with University Way—"The Ave." Like many love affairs, it began at night.

Street cars rattled and clanged most of the night. I savored walking to work at Wiseman's while overhead the night-hawks swooped, swirled, and screamed as they searched for insects. The sixteen story Meany Hotel had just been built. In its penthouse lived T. J. Murphy who hosted a theatre in the round. Hence the name of the present campus Penthouse Theatre. Occasionally I would be dispatched during my graveyard shift at Wiseman's to deliver sandwiches to a hotel room. I could gawk at its finery and perhaps at the girl who came to the door. Thirty years later I was to lead a complicated legal battle that kept the hotel from being turned into a retirement home. Today it is one of Seattle's outstanding establishments.

The Via Fontana room in the Wilsonian Hotel located on the Ave a block and a half north of Wiseman's boasted a tiled Italian fountain and decor to match. Peg belonged to the Greek Club. One night in the mid-thirties we attended its banquet after which we drove back to our shack on the beach, a memorable contrast. Today the fountain is gone, replaced by a Greek restaurant. The Wilsonian, now perhaps 70 years old and creaking at its joints, carries on, with business offices on the lower floor and residential units above, occupied mostly by retirees. It is well maintained and, given the present management, should make a contribution to the community for a long time to come.

Half a block down the Ave was the Egyptian Theatre where rotund and genial James Murphy — "Murph" — was manager. As I am reminded by Jack Pitcher, one of his former ten-year-old patrons, he was never without a cigar. At night he always stood at the theater entrance wearing a black tuxedo, warmly greeting even the smallest of his customers. He lacked only a pointed hat and feather to be a leprechaun. I first met Murph during World War II. Sensing my need to improve my speaking ability, I signed up to make a Savings Bond pitch in theaters. I was assigned to the Egyptian and therefore to Murph. Three nights a week at intermission Murph would step from the wings and introduce me with the same flourish he must have exhibited when presenting acts on the runways of burlesque houses before the talkies did them in.

After Peg and I opened a law office in the District, Murph became a rich source of theater history. We often stood in front of the Egyptian talking theater between customers. Murph liked best the Pantages downtown at Third and University—a white marble palace of a theater not unlike the one preserved in Tacoma. The stage was large enough to accommodate an animal act including elephants. It was there that in 1932 I had watched a prize fight featuring the boxer Georges Carpentier. Week after week one act followed another: comedians, jugglers, dance troupes, song and dance teams. I believe that working the Pantages had once been Murph's highest ambition.

Also downtown, the Fanchon & Marco Review with 26 dance and stage shows touring the Country was a regular, each unit spending a week amid the oriental splendor of the Fifth Avenue Theater. Eddie Peabody and his banjo were also regulars. Now the "5th" is historically preserved and in recent years hosts such musicals as *The Pajama Game*, *The King and I*, and *Chorus Line*. The Paramount with its booming organ was a latecomer to downtown. Its Revues followed much the same format as the Fifth Avenue with both movies and stage presentations. Now being given new life by remodeling, its stage could again become one of the country's best. The Moore at third and Lenora, built in 1907 with a gallery something like a steep ski slope, still sporadically operates. The immense RKO Orpheum, replaced by the Westin Hotel, played the Orpheum Circuit and purveyed both movies and stage shows. Louie Armstrong was one of the last greats to play there.

In the 1930's plays were vital to the Seattle scene. Theaters were not the intimate spaces of today but huge arenas seating hundreds. They were very much the thing for a night out. By 1940 these live playhouses with their excellent performances, most of them downtown, were closing. The Metropolitan on University Street, once wrapped around by the Olympic hotel, was a marvelous theater. It was there that Peg and I saw the musical *No No Nannette* and the play *Harvey* with Joe E. Brown and his imaginary white rabbit. Now it is the hotel's drive-in entrance. The arched opening of the Grand Opera House at 213 Cherry is bricked up and pierced by a parking garage door.

Gregarious Murph joined the Rotary Club where he became famous for droll one liners. Typical was the day the speaker was describing how to tie trout flies. Murph interrupted to solemnly advise, "I don't tie my flies. I think a zipper is preferable."

Thinking about Murph reminds me of my own youthful ventures with Bus and Willis Koch in burlesque houses on Denver's Larimer Street. We once heard a comedian called a "Peach Orchard Boar." We spent months calling each other "Peach Orchard Boars" without the slightest idea what it meant beyond sounding gratifyingly risqué.

Murph and the Egyptian are both deceased, one replaced by fading memories, and the other by a drug store and assorted small businesses some of which struggle to survive.

You will meet many characters in this book. A few in the business community stand out. One was Doc Holloway, a dentist who bought the Wilsonian Hotel on a shoe string and later lost it. Doc was an old man still practicing dentistry when I knew him. He attracted as many patients as possible for a dentist with a case of halitosis recognizable six feet away. Years before the Alaska highway was seriously considered, Doc had campaigned for its construction along the abandoned Telegraph Creek Trail. Here a telegraph line was once envisioned that would cross British Columbia, the Yukon and Alaska and end up on the shores of the Bering Sea where it would connect to an undersea cable to Europe. Work had actually gotten underway when it was announced that a cable had been laid across the Atlantic. Why not replace it with a road? Doc argued. He preached his wacky idea to anyone who would listen. Wackier yet was his campaign to pave over the quad on campus and build a parking garage underneath. The older professors such as John Condon were aghast. The tree lined walkways were sacred. Once again we labeled Doc a dreamer. But others pursued the same dream. The parking garage was built. Doc deserves a plaque on campus or at least an underground parking stall dedicated to his memory.

University Way was then advertised as "A Department Store Eight Blocks Long." No longer! A rash of new construction commenced in the 1940's, new bank buildings, a bright new Penneys and Lerners. Three five-and-dime stores, Kress, Diamond, and Woolworths all offered everything required — diapers, baby powder, decals, towels, mops, pots and pans, inexpensive clothing, sheets and pillow cases, china plates and cups, percolators — to set up or maintain a household. A bright new men's store actually sold suits and ties. Now all, except for the banks, have been washed away by a tidal wave of youth uninterested in the trappings that pleased their elders. Only the University Book Store, a few well run specialty shops including a jewelry store and a few import and craft stores, two drug stores and a hardware store stand out among dozens of eateries providing a smorgasbord of their owner's national dishes plus a collegiate tavern that would be a gem near any university.

The Limited recently closed its store on the Ave. The Gap now sells blue jeans and sweaters in University Village. At the same time, they have closed their store in the University District.

The District is still an exciting place with an atmosphere perhaps tilted too much toward drugs, panhandling, and kids who have made themselves unemployable with dye jobs, nose and lip rings, and a belligerent attitude as they demand free food and housing. I must admit to feeling a faint fatherly stirring on the few occasions I have talked to one who reciprocated. Nevertheless today they are causing many stores to consider closing or moving elsewhere. Kinkos has been a welcome addition but Godfather's Pizza has closed.

When I first enrolled at the University of Washington in 1930 it had fewer than 5000 students. The police force consisted of a constable who walked with a limp. By the middle 60's it hosted almost 30,000 students and a police force larger than one in one of O'Henry's Banana Republics.

Before my day on the Avenue, the huge, white clapboard University President's mansion stood across the alley from what is now the

University Book Store. By the time I arrived it had deteriorated into a run-down rooming house known as "Cockroach Manor." Finally it was torn down to make way for the bookstore parking lot.

In the spring of 1933 Peg and I were already plotting to elope. I took a second job with a law firm delivering papers five afternoons a week plus attending Superior Court case setting on Saturday mornings. Two things soon happened, one good, one bad. The National Recovery Act forced Dick Wiseman to increase my wage from 25 to 29 cents an hour. The law firm laid me off for a month while they determined that my 25 dollars a month job would not increase the payroll sufficiently to bring them under the N.R.A. requirements.

I probably wasn't worth much more. I am sure I must have been asleep when I fell over in the library chair. The firm took the ten dollars cost of repair out of my next check. They shall remain nameless but unpleasantly enshrined in my memory.

We arranged for a marriage license by mail. On 3 July 1933 we took the boat *Princess* to Victoria. Dick let me leave the restaurant at six a.m and return at two a.m. The law firm gave me a day off to be credited against my future vacation. At 7:30 we sailed. We found a happy and meaningful marriage that continues to this day.

In Victoria a cousin of Peg's kept us on schedule. First to the marriage bureau, then to her home where we joined her husband, three daughters and a bouquet picked in their front yard for Peg to carry, and finally to a huge church where we met Dr. Boothroyd in his study. As usual I distinguished my-

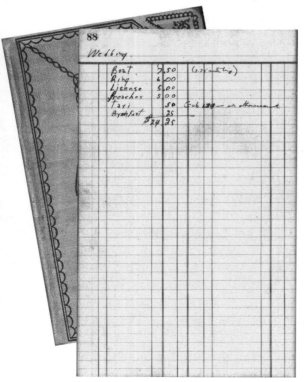

self. When he said "I want you to repeat the words after me," followed by "Now take her by the left hand," I took him literally.

Peg must have been badly disappointed. The setting sun was obscured by clouds. The boat was full. We looked wistfully at the lighted upper deck cabins. Finally we found an unoccupied bench in the bowels of the ship. I lay down and slept with my head on Peg's lap while she sat clutching her withering flowers.

Our wedding expenditures, which we carefully recorded in a ledger, totalled 25 dollars. Two round trip tickets to Victoria came to seven dollars. The marriage licence and the preacher each cost five dollars. Breakfast for the two of us cost 25 cents. The wedding ring came to six dollars. Yes, it was solid gold.

For the first year we kept track of our expenses and used a joint checking account, only to find it a source of disagreement. We ended up with two separate accounts. We divided our income, and each of us assumed responsibility for a portion of our expenses. We still do. Until this occurred we kept a ledger, which evidences both our poverty and our mad extravagances. We spent one dollar and 98 cents on a pair of shoes. Milk, cottage cheese, peaches, and hamburger each cost ten cents. Our rent came to ten dollars a month. We spent one dollar on poker chips, ten cents for ice cream, and the astronomical sum of 14 dollars and 50 cents for books (for law school).

We had planned that I would leave Wiseman's. It was not to be. Peg had a job with a private social agency that paid 50 dollars a month. When she returned to work and proudly displayed her wedding ring, she was terminated. "No married women."

Later her sociology degree earned her a position with the Welfare Department. It didn't work. She shared the woes of her caseload and was often reprimanded for her Saturday deliveries of firewood, clothing, and staples she had managed to scrounge. Finally she left to work part time in a dairy store.

For two years we had been living in a one room waterfront shack on Magnolia Bluff. We had no electricity and a faucet in the side yard. I dug an outside privy. It was a free and happy life. We loved it. The first one up in the morning would wind up our tinny phonograph and perhaps play "La Cucaracha." But Peg was pregnant. Besides, the widening crack in the clay behind the shack spelled its imminent demise.

In September, 1935 I graduated from law school. I had a choice. Leave Wiseman's or flunk the Bar Exam. I passed the Bar Exam in January, 1936. No law jobs were to be had, at least for a C+ student. I was to spend five years with the Bon Marche starting at 13 dollars and 20 cents a week. It enabled us to move to a small apartment before our daughter Leslie was born. We had a rather uncouth description of Leslie. It ran "Our little darling met a bear, the bear was bulgy. Guess who?" We brought her home from the hospital on 29 April 1937 which turned out to be a wild night. Leslie wailed and Peg fainted on the bathroom floor. I called the hospital. "No, we will not take your baby back for a few days!"

Leslie in many ways turned out to be the ideal child. She was plump and happy. From the beginning she had an inborn desire to do what she considered to be right even though she might tangle with others over its definition. Putting her to bed was difficult. She claimed an inalienable right to stay up as long as anyone was talking. Les was curious about everything. When the house we moved into a year after her birth was shaken by an earthquake at midnight she descended the stairs shouting, "I want to see the house walking." Peg's father, the one who tore up the Sunday comics, blessed her with his obstinate drive to succeed.

In 1938 we purchased a house for 150 dollars down. It perched on the side of a hill overlooking Lake Washington from the Seattle side. Below us the floating bridge was under construction. A stretch of shore line was unoccupied and a whiff of smoke occasionally broke through from sawdust buried under an old mill site. The Yesler cable car ran within walking distance to the foot ferry with its engine almost in the passenger compartment. It ran to Mercer Island and on to the mainland.

I started with the Bon Marche in the Collection Department and left five years later as the Store Manager's Assistant. The title was imposing but deceptive. My boss, Henry B. Owen, was in charge of the physical plant and non-sales personnel. Under his direction I supervised store improvements, drafted construction contracts, Oversaw our relationship with franchised departments, and looked after such operations as the delivery service and building maintenance.

It should have been fun. As it was, I developed a stomach ulcer. The whole time I knew him, my boss, Henry B. Owen, was running scared.

Walter J. Lawrie, the merchandise manager, was "King of the Hill." Owen, as operations manager, was as subject to his rages as anyone else. I have often thought that, given a free hand, Owen might have done a better job of running the store.

During the months before I myself resigned, Owen kept a resignation in his pocket, anticipating that he would someday hand it to Lawrie before Lawrie pronounced a death sentence. There had to be a final show down. I missed it by leaving but probably would have followed him out the door with Lawrie's foot mark on my rear whether he resigned or was fired.

Walter J. Lawrie was a talented but strange man. He was a hypochondriac. Shake his hand and moments later he would head for Executive Toilet to wash it off. You could hear him chastising his buyers up and down the Executive Suite, commonly referred to as Mahogany Row. His language could be vivid. During one Christmas season a record player was installed by the Display Manager in a third floor fitting room. One afternoon I encountered a lad, pale, shaking, almost crying.

"What happened?" I asked.

"I don't really know. I'm supposed to run the phonograph in a third floor fitting room. I knew I wasn't supposed to play jazz but somehow a jazz record got mixed in. A tall guy I never saw before came in. He picked up my records and threw them on the floor."

Lawrie had then shouted, "If you play another record like that you won't play anything else until Jesus Christ hands you a harp. Understand!"

Owen himself was not an easy taskmaster. I can't recall his reprimanding me but neither did he praise. He was, however, human. At one conference with several department heads I noticed his secretary sitting next to him squirming uncomfortably. Upon later inquiry it developed that he had been snapping her garter.

Often Owen and I would consider various facets of the store operation until late at night. On the way home I would frequently change street cars near midnight at 12th and Jackson where I would enjoy a brief conversation with "Old Never Sleep." He was a genial, black, one armed paper vendor who lived in an upright piano box on the corner.

One such late evening meeting gave rise to perhaps my closest call with my employer. I had come home late, exhausted after what I thought had been an unnecessarily long evening. I promptly let off steam. Leslie, almost three and as usual anxious to participate in the action, showed up in her pajamas. "What's an Owen?" she asked. I told her it was a creature half man, one-quarter lion, and the rest a fire breathing dragon.

A few days later Peg was in the store with Leslie running ahead. Les paid no attention to me sitting outside Owen's office and instead ran down mahogany row shouting repeatedly, "I want to see the Owen!" Peg collared and silenced her before either Owen or Lawrie appeared at their doors. Had Lawrie known the entire story he probably would have called Les in for a conference.

Cal Jr. showed up in 1939. Like Les he grew up fearless around water. Unlike Les, who now travels the world buying for her craft shop on the Ave and who thrives on danger, Cal Jr. is more concerned with longevity except when on the water or climbing mountains. Like Les he has never caused his parents concern except for such problems as getting lost with two friends in a blizzard near the 10,000 foot level on Mt. Rainier. The guides were sure they were dead. I persuaded them to brave the weather and at least go up as far as Camp Muir. Instead of hiking across the glacier and into a crevasse as the guides predicted, they had carved out a cave in the snow.

In 1940, war was on the horizon and there was a demand for lawyers, at least one who, with a stomach ulcer, was unlikely to be drafted.

I spurned a substantial raise from the Bon Marche and went with Jones & Bronson. It was my first taste of a pleasant and understanding law firm. I had a wonderful time and gained valuable experience but by mid-1945 the old hands were returning. Peg and I opened our own office on the Ave.

Chapter 3

The Rolling Main and Beyond

In the summer of 1942 we bought our boat, the *Anna Lou*, and for nine years lived aboard her with our two children and our schnauzer. Peg claims that from the Government Locks to the Port Madison spit the bottom of Puget Sound is strewn with her best china because I let the *Anna Lou* roll in the trough when that was the shortest course. Living on a boat satisfied both our pocketbook and a yearning for adventure. I had already been rejected by the draft (stomach ulcer) and cursorily turned down by the Navy (bad eyes). We arrived at owning the *Anna Lou* in stages by wetting our feet a little at a time with a smaller boat.

Opposite: At home on the Anna Lou. Peg, Leslie, and Mac, early 1940's.

The water attracted us long before we lived on it. Lugging Leslie Grace and Cal Jr., with Patty the dog foraging ahead looking for a fight, we made frequent trips down the hill to the shore of Lake Washington and along the shore to Seaborne's Marina near the ferry landing. It was there we found the *Whimsy*, a clumsy, arthritic little 22 foot craft with a fan tail and a one lung engine,

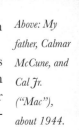

by our standards quite loveable. I borrowed 275 dollars from the Bon Marche Credit Union and it was ours.

Above: My father, Calmar McCune, and Cal Jr. ("Mac"), about 1944.

We kept our house for another two years but took frequent trips on the *Whimsy*. Leslie slept on one bunk, and Peg slept on the cabin floor. We housed one-year-old Cal Jr. in a plywood box on the other bunk. Except when it was raining I curled up around the engine housing in the stern.

Once, out on Hood Canal, we courted disaster. A storm blew up and just then the engine gave a final wheeze and died. A frantic search disclosed that the baby Cal Jr. had reached up from his box and pulled the engine switch.

Except for two other matters the Hood Canal voyage was uneventful. On July 3rd I forgot our ninth wedding anniversary. All that day Peg looked forlorn. I was unsure why until the next day when she inquired if I remembered the day of the month. Equally painful was a sunburn that left me for two days with an eye slitted paper bag over my head. After that we pretty much stayed on Lake Washington.

At that time Bellevue consisted of open fields and orchards. There were two stores, one above Meydenbauer Bay, the other about where the Bellevue Mall is now. We walked to it many times. The shore of the Bay was deserted except for a small, rather unkept park with swings. Farther along three rusting whaling ships were mothballed. I suspect they ended up as salvage.

It was clear we were happiest on the water. Besides, housing prices had risen. We sold the equity in our home and most of our furniture and for 1800 dollars bought the *Anna Lou*, a Lake Union Dream Boat. She was 40 feet long with a 12 foot beam, built in 1928. To steady her, the bilge had been poured full of concrete. Once at a banquet I sat next to the owner of Shepard Ambulance. He told me that he had once owned the *Anna Lou*. He'd put her up for sale the day after he dreamed that in a storm the concrete had fallen through the hull.

When she was underway a rubber flap covered the opening of the head. At the moorage fish often swam in the bowl. We hand-pumped water to flush the toilet into a tank. In salt water when the flushing mechanism was tripped, the bowl often glowed with a cascade of phosphorescence.

When we purchased the *Anna Lou* our enthusiasm surpassed our good sense. A boat we had, but no place for permanent moorage. "What about the Seattle Yacht Club?" Peg hazarded. We stopped momentarily at the entrance. Intimidated by the sign "MEMBERS ONLY" on a stately white column, I started to drive away. From outside the car we heard a loud wail. Leslie had opened the rear door and fallen out on her head.

First aid was essential. We entered the Club House. While Peg took Leslie to the restroom I struck up a conversation with Hutch, the

The Whimsey and its successor, the Anna Lou.

manager. Almost incidentally, I recounted our problem. "Of course you can live on board, many members love doing so." I paid an initiation fee of 25 dollars (currently 7500 dollars). The next day we commenced a ten year stay in stall 10 on the north pier. I assume the trustees gave their approval retroactively. Most vessels had been taken for government use and the docks were almost empty. We were probably approved by a voice vote.

As a member of the family our dog Patty deserves a word. She loved to roll in rotting fish and never enjoyed the taste of dog food. Her favorite dish was anything she could catch and kill herself. This included, when we lived in the house, the neighbors' gold fish which we of course vehemently denied. Just to check I brought home 10 cents worth of gold fish and put them in a wash tub. It was a disappearing act, one gulp for each.

We acquired Patty in the following way. Peg had been working in a dairy store when Patty's owner came in and asked to use the phone. She wanted to call the pound and get rid of her dog. Instead, Peg made an appointment for us to pick up the unwanted critter. We arrived at five o'clock. Patty was gone. The owner whistled from her front porch. A grey streak ran toward us from up the block. An angry gentleman came out on the sidewalk.

"Why don't you keep your damn chicken-killing dog tied up?" Patty was obviously just our type. A few weeks later it turned out that she was pregnant. It would be difficult to remember the number of times this occurred or the number of friends we lost giving away pups with all their mother's instincts plus a paternal side which may have been worse.

When we moved to the *Anna Lou* we established Patty in a dog house lashed to the foredeck. Years later she had a heart attack and we had no choice but to put her to sleep. We tearfully buried her in her dog house near the home we were then building a few blocks away. Unfortunately her mausoleum was hit by a bulldozer and graded into the lot. Plant a tree and you were likely to be reminded of Patty. She would have loved it.

Patty's greatest victory was in the public park which abutted the end of our pier. A nearby resident owned a hugh police dog called "Lady" that also frequented the park. Patty would follow Lady growling at what often proved to be an unsafe distance. On two occasions we paid the vet to sew her up. After their final encounter we let her mend on her own.

I was on board when I heard the uproar. Grabbing an empty glass bottle I ran down the dock. Lady's owner had her by the collar and was trying to shake Patty's head out of Lady's mouth. I whacked Lady over the head with the bottle and before I could drag Patty away she nipped Lady under her foreleg. Weeks later I ran into Lady's owner.

"How's Lady?"

"She's dead. Your dog bit her and it got infected." Patty in the meantime had healed on her own. Lady's owner was not interested.

Leslie and baby Mac in the kitchen of our first house.

Much more lovable was Happy, a dog I acquired in the stock market and brought home to live with us on the *Anna Lou*. I first saw Happy, a little brownish yellow dog, in the lobby of the 1411 4th Avenue Building. When I took the elevator to an upper floor Happy boarded as well. She wandered off alone on a floor then occupied by a local stock market. I kept my appointment but had difficulty putting the little yellow dog out of my mind. Going back down I asked the elevator operator if she had seen the dog?

"No I haven't. I thought it was with someone or I would never have let it on the elevator."

A quick search of the stock market turned up Happy going from person to person. Obviously she was lost and seeking a friend. I scooped her up. She nestled into my arms and into the life of the McCunes.

Unlike Patty, Happy sought only to love and be loved. Scold her and if you were sitting she would jump onto your lap. Her favorite activity was to bring rocks to be thrown over the house we were building and into the adjoining woods. She would then run around the house and proudly and invariably bring back the same rock. She moved with us to the house when it was completed. We parted reluctantly only when she became both blind and deaf.

We moved to the *Anna Lou* in the summer of 1942. The United States had already declared war. I confess that the war only made life more interesting. For instance, the *Anna Lou* had an upright oil burning heater in the cabin and an oil burner in the galley stove. The foibles of the bureaucracy dictated that oil was taboo. But for some reason, perhaps because I had taken out a license to fish for dog fish— vitamin A and oil for precision instruments was extracted from their livers—our gasoline supply for use on the boat was unlimited. We installed an airtight wood burning stove and remodeled the galley to burn wood. Almost every weekend during the winter we took off to pick up wood on vacant beaches that are now lined with houses. We were prohibited from taking cameras out on Puget Sound. We checked them at the Government locks that provide access from Seattle's lakes to Puget Sound. We were permitted a shotgun and 50 rounds of ammunition.

We spent many Christmases anchored in the almost deserted inner harbor at Port Madison at the North end of Bainbridge Island. A store operated at the entrance. In front of the store was a rock reef consisting of stone carried as ballast by sailing ships. Ships used to jettison the stone before loading lumber at the Port Madison saw mill, no sign of which remains.

After the war our forays lengthened. We usually sailed first to Roche Harbor, a sheltered bay at the northwest corner of San Juan Island. Roche proved to be the ideal departure point for our many voyages into the Canadian San Juans. Possessed of vast lime deposits, it had been the personal fiefdom of a crusty Scotchman named John S. McMillin. The English had first mined the lime during their occupancy of that portion of San Juan Island. When the boundary question was settled in 1872 all of San Juan Island was awarded to the United States. McMillin, an American, acquired all other interests in the Roche Harbor lime deposits. In 1886 he formed the Roche Harbor Lime and Cement Company, with himself in firm control.

Until the early 1950's McMillin's kilns growled and glowed day and night. They furnished most of the cement that glued together the buildings of early Seattle and San Francisco. Indeed, for almost 20 years McMillin enjoyed a virtual monopoly on the lime business west of the Mississippi. But by 1940 orders were dwindling as more convenient and perhaps less expensive sources were developed. In 1956 the fires went out. Back in 1896 McMillin had built the famous De Haro Hotel. By the time we arrived the two story vine covered hotel had been closed since 1942 and was showing signs of dilapidation. Many of the company owned houses stood empty. McMillin had died in 1936. Roche waited to be resurrected as a marina and resort community.

The most indelible reminder of McMillin's supremacy is the family mausoleum a short walk up a nearby hill. Tall Grecian-looking stone columns are set in a circle. Inside the circle, cement chairs ring a stone table. Inserted into each chair seat is a plate that could be removed to accept the ashes of a family member or at least some token of their existence. One chair is missing. The column at its back is broken off. The bottom is gone and the top portion dangles over the missing seat from the overhead band of stone that connects the columns. It is said that the structure with its stairways, columns, and inscriptions represents several organizations to which McMillin belonged; primarily the Masons but also the Sigma Chi fraternity.

McMillin did not live to complete the mausoleum. He planned it to be capped with a bronze dome and had ordered the dome from a Virginia firm. His son Paul, citing the company's financial condition, cancelled the order. This antagonized McMillin and damaged their already unhappy relationship. Of the children, at least Paul's remains are buried elsewhere. But even without the dome the mausoleum is a startling sight to come upon in the woods.

At that time the present busy restaurant that overlooks the bay had only a caretaker. On one occasion we anchored directly in front and while Peg remonstrated me over my intention to throw our garbage over the side, the caretaker came out on the balcony and emptied a garbage can onto the beach below.

Our *Anna Lou* was often the only vessel anchored in the harbor. Today at Roche yachts crowd the docks and conviviality fills the air. In the Canadian San Juan Islands too, moorages dot the harbors. I can't criticize. What else can a boat lover do in a day when quiet anchorages are difficult to find and the wake of a passing boat can call you on deck in the middle of the night to see if the anchor is dragging.

Table and chair in the McMillin mausoleum.

North of a treacherous stretch of open ocean, from Christie Passage at the north end of Vancouver Island to the shelter of Fitzhugh Sound some thirty miles away, lonely moorages can still be found. This too may end. Palatial yachts loaded with electronics make the search for adventure that only privacy can bring more difficult. Even for smaller vessels navigation has been simplified. A depth sounder, radar, and radio communication are still essential. Are you lost in the fog? For less than 900 dollars you can purchase a device called a G.P.S.. Held in the palm of the hand, it automatically triangulates signals from satellites and will tell you where you are within a few feet, almost anywhere in the world.

For the past 40 years Peg and I have been blessed with an equally close relationship with Dean and Joy Worcester and their five children. Our boating adventures often included them. Dean, an economics professor, was and is a skinny blond from Lincoln, Nebraska who, even then used a cane and fought off severe arthritis. Joy is the tightly wound daughter of Czech immigrants. She graduated from the University of Nebraska with Dean. Both fight off inactivity as if it were a dread disease. Dean, now retired, has had four hip replacements. Today he mows the lawn, participates at the state level in the health care program and he is writing a book. After she raised her children, Joy taught for 15 years in the Seattle Public Schools. Her current projects are volunteering several days a week at the University Hospital, organizing seminars for first time mothers, and tending a garden of almost an acre.

Once, out on the Straits with Dean and Joy, we ran into trouble. The boat was rolling dangerously in tide rips off Port Townsend. Our destination, Victoria B.C., lay somewhere ahead in a fog bank. Dean asked, rather pointedly, "Just what are we doing out here anyway?" I was at a loss for an answer. Between two "big ones" I successfully put about and we ran for the shelter of Whidby Island.

Leslie and Cal Jr. were never on the deck or pier without a life belt until they grew older and became good swimmers. Aside from insisting on this we never told them to be afraid of falling in. Indeed, on our first day aboard the *Anna Lou*, I was coming home just as three-year-old Les walked off the pier into the lake while carrying garbage up shore. Her coat hid her life belt and since I didn't want to take a chance I jumped in myself. Peg helped us both out and we made light of our swim.

When they were older Peg usually escorted the children to and from school. We warned them only that they were to stay clear of "Barnacle Bill" Headley if his face was red. Barnacle Bill was a former professional violinist who lived alone in his sailboat *The Sinbad* and gave music lessons. A crusty character, he was outspoken when sober, but at his blasphemous best after a bout with the bottle. Bill was revered by the other Club members as an historical monument. Beyond nodding hello I can't recall talking to him. Bill wasn't dangerous but on more than one occasion upon sighting Les or Cal Jr. he would shout soothing remarks like "They're turning the Club into a goddamn kindergarten."

I remember Leslie sitting on the pier examining the sterns of two

adjoining sail boats bearing the names "Sonny" and "Irene." After peering earnestly down through the clear water at their rudders and propellers for several minutes she looked up and asked, "What's the difference between a girl boat and a boy boat?" Try that one on for size.

At the age of 11 Cal Jr. acquired the plans for a racing speed boat. No chance of building it until we moved to a house. Eventually we built it in the attic. It was an eight foot bomb shell. Peg insisted on trying it out near the Yacht Club. She almost killed herself. Pounding the racing throttle she frantically tried to shut off the engine as the boat roared toward shore. She succeeded within ten feet of disaster.

The years on the *Anna Lou* were precious. But by l948 it was obvious that our children needed bedrooms. Leslie had a doll collection that would fill a room. Cal Jr. collected match books and he wanted to build the speed boat. Most of our live-aboard friends had already gone ashore. The increasing sophistication of the Seattle Yacht Club also spelled an end to our dream. We decided to build a house.

My building experience had consisted of building "A" shaped hog houses and digging caves. Not good selling points when asking a bank, that much later was glad to loan me 160,000 dollars unsecured, to provide 8000 dollars to buy a lot and build a 2500 square foot house. Bill Wagner, an investor and fellow Rotarian who liked me was willing to take a chance. He loaned us 8000 dollars.

With his loan we bought a lot for 2000 dollars a few blocks away, prepared our own plans, and went to work. Don't try it today. The Building Department will hold you up for months and at great expense supervise every nail you pound. But then, perhaps because of our enthusiastic youth, they helped us in every way possible. They, like all of us, are now caught up in the bureaucratic maze.

Peg and I worked on the house nights and weekends except when I took a day off to pour concrete. Les and Cal Jr. were efficient mixers of mortar when it came to laying concrete blocks below grade and insulating blocks above.

Finally we put in the rafters. In the process Peg fell between them and landed stern first. She still complains that I didn't ask if she was hurt but simply commanded, "Get up." I was too scared to be rational.

Eventually we finished the house, thanks in substantial part to a sympathetic neighbor, Ed Doolittle, who watched me laboring with a hand saw and brought over an old Skill Saw.

If the red tape could be untangled anyone willing to devote the time and energy could duplicate our efforts today. I was to be active for a number of years on the Seattle Planning Commission and before that on the Housing Advisory Board. Nothing gave me more pleasure than the Yesler Atlantic project which sought to improve the housing in a portion of the Central Area. I was amazed by the desire of the Blacks to improve their housing under, it is true, duress of the housing code, which they seemed to regard as an opportunity. The danger was that they might be taken advantage of by unscrupulous contractors. For a couple of years we had funds from the City to hire a building expert. His presence made it possible for many owners to carry out work which otherwise would have been a financial burden for years.

Perhaps I have wandered from my point. Our experience led me to the conclusion that the easiest money you can make is by doing work yourself. You aren't spending after-tax income, you avoid the contractor's labor cost, overhead, and profit, and it's fun. Peg and I built six more houses. Some things I wouldn't try, such as plumbing and installing electrical lines located within the floor and walls. Installation of fixtures is no problem if one is reasonably handy. In suburbia only a qualified contractor can install your septic tank system. A Skill saw is a great tool and trim will cover many defects. You must also be cognizant of the areas where expert assistance is required.

In the early fifties I argued and barely won a picketing case before the United States Supreme Court that clipped the wings of an overly zealous Union. The union was demanding that my client, who operated a three-man used car lot, either refrain from selling or else pay the commission to one of his salesmen. Justice Black and I had a rather heated exchange and I won by a four to four decision which was enough to sustain the lower Court's ruling. Had Justice William O. Douglas not been on vacation I would have lost.

I made nothing from my venture into the heady atmosphere of the Supreme Court, but our finances were looking up. I was elected President of my University District Rotary Club and along with Peg attended the International Convention in Paris in 1953. It was then that I visited Ireland and saw the ruins of my great grandfather Bell's property.

In 1955 I learned to fly. Until I failed to pass the physical in 1992 at the age of eighty-one, I flew by myself and with Gene and Dollie Glasson in our "Club" plane, first a Cessna 172 and then a 1961 182. We flew thousands of miles. From Seattle we winged north and east across the Canadian tundra to watch the ice break up and the polar bears scavenging the garbage dump at Hudson Bay. Once we flew to the outer Bahamas with false reassurance provided by the fact that we could see the ocean bottom most of the way. We flew numerous times to Mexico, where we became familiar with remote air fields and sometimes with Mexican Customs officials. We would fly in and out of uncontrolled airports and show up at customs days later. Several times we illegally flew with a single engine plane directly from the tip of Baja, over the gulf of Cortez, to Los Mochis. Well aware of the genteel poverty of the Customs officers, we tipped generously, never thinking of it as a mordida—a bribe, which it was not. Incidentally, on our final trip to Mexico we found its flight controllers and navigation aids much like those in the United States. On our first trips there was little communication between airports and weather prediction was often limited to whether the barometer was going up or down.

Once, after de-icing we took off from Rock Springs, Wyoming after a two day freezing, snowy weather delay. We landed at Havasu, Arizona, home of the old, reassembled London Bridge. It was 80 degrees. Gene and I each wore two pairs of wool pants, long underwear, several shirts and sheepskin coats. Dolly had wrapped herself in blankets.

Peg didn't like to fly with me. Something about an "unconscious death wish."

Once I rented a Cessna and flew Dean Worcester and his daughter

Mary over Bagio in the Philippines. On the return we found ourselves above a dense cloud cover when the Manila VOR went out. This is a navigational device usually stationed near an airport, that provides a heading to steer the plane. Without such a compass bearing to home in on we were forced to rely on our plane's own uncertain compass headings and could easily have flown out over the Pacific. Fortunately I spotted a hole and spiraled down through.

A great adventure in the fifties was again on the water—the voyage of the *Eastward Spade*. Cal Jr. called her that since she was the reverse of the "Westward Ho." In the fall of 1957 Cal came home full of enthusiasm for a converted Japanese life boat he could buy for 600 dollars out of his summer earnings as a gardener. He wanted to sail it to Alaska. Certain that it would kill the deal, I suggested he offer 400 dollars. The owner gratefully accepted.

I surveyed his find. She had never been taken out of her shipping cradle. Eighteen feet on the water line her huge concrete keel would have pulled her down in seconds had she filled. A Japanese-type poop deck extended several feet beyond her stern post. On the deck the mast and the boom were tangled in a rat's nest of rotting rigging. Digging through the mess and opening the hatches we found a rusty Japanese one cylinder engine occupying the stern. In the cabin was a Japanese oil lamp set in gimbals and the port and starboard kerosene burning running lights. The sails stored in dunnage bags were in good condition. There was no head, then or later. Just sit on the edge of the poop deck like on the old sailing ships or use a bucket when there might be onlookers.

Cal Jr.'s enthusiasm proved contagious. We caulked the seams and soon she was tied up in an adjoining vacant moorage at the Club. We planned it as a joint project. Cal would do most of the work. I would supply a new engine and rigging. On 1 May 1959 we chugged off toward Alaska. With our nine horsepower, air-cooled Briggs & Stratton engine made to power a garden tractor echoing off the walls of the locks, the lock gates opened. The *Eastward Spade* was outward bound. We waved good-bye to our family and friends above. Peg, I am sure, wished she was along. Leslie, in tears, thought we were gone for good. She was almost right.

Delayed by engine problems, it took us two days to reach Coronet Bay located just inside Deception Pass. The pass lies at the northern tip of Whidby Island and provides entrance to the straits of San Juan de Fuca. When the tides change it is as if a huge bathtub stopper has been pulled. When the tide comes in the Pacific Ocean races to fill Puget Sound and when it goes out the Sound disgorges itself into the ocean. The rips, tides, and currents in Deception Pass can run over 7 knots and the immense whirlpools and steep rock walls can be treacherous. Much of Puget Sound ebbs and flows through this narrow gap in the rocks. Beyond are the Straits of San Juan De Fuca and a course can be set for Roche Harbor or a safer one to Cattle Point, both in the American San Juans. The seas outside the pass can be wicked or smooth and it is best to know beforehand what you will find. You will enjoy the brisk smell of the sea untainted by forests or the hand of man.

The *Eastward Spade*, doing three and one half knots at full throttle, could only make it through the pass near the slack. Anxious to catch the slack before the outgoing tide began I arose at five and sleepily cranked the engine. It backfired. The crank flew off and knocked me out momentarily, breaking my nose.

The ruckus woke Cal Jr. "Got to get you to a doctor." He started the engine and hoisted the anchor. It was almost slack water in the pass and he headed through.

There was no doctor available on Orcas Island. The throbbing and bleeding had stopped. We found a mirror and I pushed most of the budging side back in place. On to Sidney, B.C.

At the Sidney Customs they had no doctor to suggest. "Oh, heck! Lets go on." Forty years later Doctors were still urging that it must constrict my breathing and I should have it reamed out. They are welcome to do so at the autopsy.

We were now using both power and sail much of the time. The sails added little speed but did steady the boat. Sails alone were slower but delightful. On the way back we spent a beautiful moonlit night sailing silently across Dixon entrance, a channel lying between the Queen Charlotte Islands and Alaska that extends outward to the open Pacific ocean. Occasionally one of us will now remark to the other, "I wish we'd shot that whale." While sailing across Dixon we found ourselves coasting beside a very dead and badly bloated whale tangled in a fish net. We debated tacking back and trying to pop it with a rifle shot but held our course.

Looking back on our adventures, it was almost as if we were reen-

Totem pole at Alert Bay, British Columbia.

acting Robinson Crusoe or perhaps Gulliver's Travels.

Broughton Strait for instance. This is a long narrow channel running north beyond the treacherous Seymour Narrows with its underwater rock pinnacle not yet neutered by a mighty dynamite blast far under its base. Broughton Strait ends at the north end of Vancouver Island. It is most dangerous when the wind blows up or down the channel. We experienced this first hand. A roaring gale brought a following sea that first lifted the *Eastward Spade* high then sped onward, abandoning her to slide down stern first from the foaming crest into a nasty trough. Both of us must have thought about the chunk of concrete bolted to her belly each time she almost fell off broadside into the trough. We could easily have been finished off by a following wave. The Gulliver part came after we rounded a point on Cormorant Island and began coasting at half throttle over the quiet waters of Alert Bay, British Columbia. Behind us the rollers were still frothing hungrily in the Strait.

A fearsome array of totem poles rose beyond the shore. In the foreground was a busy Indian community. The three-and-a-half-mile long island is home base for the Kwakiutl Indian tribe. As we anchored beyond low tide, two diesel taxis dragging tin cans and paper streamers clattered madly down the road along the shore.

Full of shouting Indians, the taxis disappeared over a rise and in a moment reappeared only to vanish again at the other end of the Island. It could only be the Kwakiutl version of a midwest chivaree where during the wedding friends do all they can to decorate and all but disable the groom's car. This is followed by a horn blowing parade that ends only when the bride and groom reach their destination.

We rowed ashore and entered the trading store crammed with odds and ends required for wilderness living. Open boxes and barrels of candies, cookies, beans, potatoes and other edibles lined the floor in front of the counter. Treated cordage and canvas contributed to a creosote-like odor as did crab traps and fishing gear hung from ceiling beams. The smell of coffee from a huge coffee grinder mixed with that of kerosene dripping from a drum. Pots, pans, and china had their place on shelves together with heavy-weather clothing including boots. In one corner a women's and girls' department brightened the room.

"Is there any Indian dancing in Alert Bay?" Cal Jr. asked the clerk.

"Don't think so."

We were at the door when the diesel taxis clattered by.

The clerk called after us. "Might try the Community Hall. There's a wedding reception there tonight. Might be some dancing."

At 8:30 we climbed the community hall steps. A burley Indian, wearing a shinny suit, father of either the bride or groom, filled the doorway. From behind him came the sound of drumming and chanting.

"We wondered——."

"Come on in." No accent, just the soft precise English of the Indian Boarding School. Shaking our hands as if we were visitors from another tribe, he steered us to a tier of seats normally used for athletic events. The only other white person sat some distance away.

At one end of the hall the wedding party sat on a raised platform with a canopy and silkish pink side curtains. Seated on a stool and higher than the others was the rather pretty bride dressed, as I recall, in a sheer orange dress. She was smoking nervously. The groom wore a flower and succeeded well in his efforts to look manly.

At the far end a long wooden plank extended between two saw horses. Six men on each side of the plank were beating out a rhythm with sticks. At one end a bass drum boomed its approval. There were no masks or headdresses.

When we came in they were chanting a haunting, high-pitched refrain that probably carried them back to the time when Alert Bay had an Indian name and the white man had not yet rounded Cormorant Point in 1844 on a steam powered paddle sloop assigned to patrol duty for the British. The British had given little Cormorant Island the ship's name.

Dancers circled the floor doing what they chose. One old man stood out. He was wearing dungarees topped by long underwear. He bobbed around the room barefoot, keeping time with the chanters and the drum. I wondered if he was dancing with his ancestors in the long house.

There were no speakers and there was no alcohol. Little boys and girls darted excitedly among the dancers. Finally the music quieted. Everyone looked around expectantly. The bass drum gave a final boom and the kitchen doors opened.

A brief word about the history of the Potlatch. A ceremony with its origin lost in time, it is sometimes credited with having been the backbone of the Indian economic system. Periodically a chief or influential tribal member would celebrate his wealth and good fortune by giving much of it away at a great festival which could include other tribes. This was the Potlatch. Such redistribution of wealth must have raised expectations for possible wealth by the recipients and also served to even out the economy.

The Great White Father in Ottawa disagreed. The Potlatch was frowned upon. Finally, the Canadian government banned it from 1894 to the mid-fifties. The incident I am recounting took place in 1959 and reflected little of the original rituals and none of the masked activity now or historically associated with the Potlatch. It did herald the return of the Potlatch to the Indian way of life.

The kitchen doors opened as the dancing stopped. Giggling and shoving, the boys and girls formed separate lines. Women, perhaps a committee that included their mothers, appeared on the floor. They gave each little girl a multicolored handkerchief and each boy a quarter. Waiving their handkerchiefs and clutching their quarters the children spread around the room obviously waiting for the next event. It came quickly.

The women again emerged from the kitchen, this time carrying a box of rayon scarves colored red, blue, green, purple, yellow and orange. They gave one to each woman who wrapped it around her shoulders. The celebration blossomed into color.

In teams of three, women now emerged from the kitchen. Two carried a washboiler piled high with sandwiches. If you are under 60 I should explain that washboilers were and in remote areas still are long oval tubs used to wash clothes. Filled with water, clothes, and soap, they were heated on top of the kitchen range. The third group of women carried paper sacks. To each man they gave a sack of sandwiches. We protested but they insisted upon giving one to each of us. As I recall only the men received the sandwiches.

Out on the floor men and women began to cluster in separate groups, the men obviously talking about the weather, fishing, or perhaps logging. Occasionally a story, no doubt on the rare side, would generate a guffaw. The women too were talking about the things that interest women everywhere. Suddenly it struck me as being not much different than an oyster feed at the Methodist Tabernacle in Haxtun, Colorado.

Now our host passed among the guests handing an envelope to each man. Refusal would have been an insult. In a few minutes we shook hands with our host and wished the married couple well. It was clear that he wanted nothing more than that we share in his good fortune.

As we left he came to the door, put a large calloused hand on my shoulder and thanked us for coming. By then it was dark. Not city darkness but only the dark that a moonless night and tall trees can bring. It either awes or frightens. Given the totem poles just visible against the sky we felt a little of each. Occasionally we passed a dimly lit house and a barking dog. In the clearings stars blazed overhead as they do in the northern latitudes. Phosphorus glowed in the wake of the dingy and dripped from the oars. Beneath the surface fish left streaks of light.

We lit the kerosene lamp, stowed the sandwiches, and opened the envelopes. In each we found four dollars Canadian. Bedding down we said little. It was time for reflection.

In Ketchican, Alaska, Cal Jr. lined up a job at a fish packing plant at Tokeen on Prince of Wales Island. Sailing north we went through some of the most beautiful scenery and waterways in the world. Then I flew out and Cal spent the summer cleaning fish. I returned in late August for the three week trip back to Seattle.

I don't frighten easily but when I do my saliva disappears. This occurred several times during my life but the worst was on the return trip. We were making an incredibly lonely night-run down Clarence Strait toward Ketchican, the hub of southeastern Alaska. The sea was "lumpy," as the fishermen say. It was overcast, after midnight, and pitch black. A drizzle obscured any beacon that would have signaled shelter. Ahead a rocket pierced the gloom and for a moment glowed

red, high in the murk. We steered toward it with water sloshing over the bow. We never sighted the source. Momentarily the drizzle thinned and we made out a navigation light. On that stretch of deserted coast it could only be the entrance to Meyers Chuck. In minutes we were sheltered behind an outcropping of rock.

I felt we had beaten the odds when two weeks later we docked at the Seattle Yacht Club.

We kept the *Anna Lou* until 1953 when we bought the *Viking*, a 1928 version of an express cruiser and an ex-rum runner.

Our trip pretty much rang down the 1960's. A year later we did make a second run to Alaska, this time with Peg helping to crew and the sturdy *Viking* underneath powered by my home-made conversion of a Chevrolet engine. All went well.

It was 1960 and in a few years would be time to tend the fires beginning to rage in Seattle.

Chapter 4

Run Up the Storm Flag

I n the pages of this book you will encounter a host of organizations and their members, as well as lone individuals, who sought to change the course of life on University Way, "the Ave," the main street running near the University of Washington. During the sixties the Ave, like our country and the world, began to fray at the seams.

It is perhaps time to provide a partial program of the players and the games they played and sought to win.

Among the first organizations to appear was the University District Movement (UDM) in 1967. It enlisted the support of street people, hippies, and students. It mounted an attack against the business community that was savage and disruptive. It was a brain child largely nurtured by Robbie Stern and his wife Suzi, Jack and Sally Delay, and Walt Crowley, then a reporter on the underground paper, *The Helix*. Its thrust was to embarrass and disrupt the Avenue establishment by seeking to right a series of wrongs they alleged we were committing. They never revealed what I believe to be their real motives. It is possible that they would still deny them.

Andy Shiga (1919-1993).

Robbie Stern, a 24 year old, heavy set, aggressive, first-year law student, acted as spokesman. He blamed the merchants for recent drug and obscenity arrests and for the closing of hippie hangouts. At the same time he argued that students were being overcharged and were entitled to discounts. Stern was destined to pass the bar and to employ his many talents in other causes. His wife Suzy was a radicalized go go dancer. Eventually they were divorced and later, according to Walt Crowley, Suzy died of a drug overdose.

Jack and Sally Delay were recent arrivals to Seattle. Their appearance on the local scene was brief and some might say tragic. I did not know them. One or both may have attended a meeting in my office. If so, I was too worked up to take notes. They operated the "Bookworm," a combination of a liberal bookstore, a reading room, and a place to argue or to take a nap. The Bookworm was, I concluded, the reason for all the fireworks.

Paul Dorpat (above); Walt Crowley.

Walt Crowley is a name to remember as you read this book. Long haired with a wispy goatee, Walt was a college dropout barely old enough to shave. His father, an engineer, worked at Boeing. As far as I know he invented the basic hovercraft, the device that scoots over water on a bubble of air. I found his mother to be a delightful but ultra-liberal intellectual who had stuffed her dropout son full of liberal learning and sent him forth to battle. I think Walt was a Trotskyist. If so, he has mellowed. In 1964 he cut high school classes to listen to Norman Thomas. (Peg gave Thomas the only vote he received in our precinct.) Walt possesses an amazing ability both to write and to draw. Some argue that he takes conflicting sides simply for the challenge. Others claim that, being in the public relations business, he's for hire. In any event, unlike Dale Carnegie, he appears more interested in "influencing people" than in "making friends." Our relationship was and still is one of fondness garnished with suspicion.

I doubt if Walt ever marched in a parade. I imagine him sitting in a smoky room helping to hatch disruptive plans. After observing the results he would return to *The Helix* to critique them in the newspaper, probably his goal all along.

Walt's forte is writing the history of organizations ranging from the staid Rainier Club, which until a few years ago had a separate side entrance for women, to the Blue Moon Tavern. He found his niche in the course of preparing a history of the Municipal League, which he undertook to comply with a Court order that he work off 900 dollars worth of parking tickets by performing public service.

Mercurial Jan Tissot will also be a frequent visitor to these pages. Jan was a skinny, tall, long-haired 30 year-old who wore granny glasses. A principal figure in the 1968 riots, he wrote poetry and goaded the capitalist system. Jan later graduated from law school but was never admitted to the Bar. Personally I thought he had the balloon-puncturing qualities of a good liberal lawyer. Whether he didn't pass the bar exam because of his grades or because of his participation in the post office bombing I never knew. Now Jan is an investigator for a governmental agency and works closely with the police. He still writes poetry and his recent book *Crow Speaks* is excellent and reflects Jan's struggle within himself.

John Matsulas.

I find it difficult to visualize Paul Dorpat as the fire-brand editor of *The Helix*. Today he is probably Seattle's leading historical photographer and philosopher with thousands of old and more recent pictures to draw upon including a few in this book. Paul wears a droopy black felt hat which conceals an immense bald head with a large clump of hair often shooting skyward on each side. A formidable presence indeed.

Crowley, Dorpat, and Tissot, and others I will refer to in this and subsequent chapters are to me good examples of why there is every hope for a young radical and far less for a drug addict.

On the business side two men stand out — John Mitsules and Andy Shiga. John, a pudgy Greek, managed a hip clothing store for men and boys. John is a Viet Nam veteran and often carried a '38 revolver. It was his genius to be able to cultivate respect and good relations with both hippies and city officials as well as the police. When we were in trouble it was his finger that went into the dike.

Andy Shiga was John's mirror image. A Japanese American, he

had been a pacifist even before World War II. Sensing trouble, he dropped out of Whitman College and during the war performed jobs such as gardening in the Midwest, thereby avoiding the hysteria against Japanese Americans that sent thousands to internment camps following Pearl Harbor.

When I first met Andy he was operating a store selling knitting equipment on the lower Ave. He was spending most of his time playing Go. To anyone who would listen he would proclaim he was holding his income to a non-taxable level rather than contribute to armaments. How, you may ask, did Andy then become the owner of more frontage on the Avenue than any another person or corporation, including the large and prosperous University Book Store?

Don't second guess the power of love which burned like a beacon in Andy's life until his death in 1993.

One day Andy dropped into my office, as he often did. "Cal, I've got a problem." He explained that he was in love with Toshimo, a Japanese girl who had to return to Japan in a few days. We discussed the impact marriage would have on Andy's lifestyle. It would mean becoming a business man, the least of his ambitions. He once characterized my fellow Rotarians as a "bunch of road apples," to which I testily responded that the Rotary Student Exchange Program was larger by far than all the others combined.

Our conference ended with a smiling Andy saying, "You think it's a good idea?"

"Best you've had in a long time," I replied.

I sometimes shudder to think their happy union might have gone the other way.

The Annual Street Fair, a gala event of crafts, music, food and entertainment, was dreamed up by Andy, with the help of Toshimo I am sure. During the riots he was a peacemaker. Without his help the University District Center (UDC), a no-drug, club-like shelter that helped young people find support and understanding, would probably have failed. In an indirect way Andy, Toshimo, and their three sons have fulfilled his search for peace.

On the University side Ernest Conrad, Vice President for Business and Finance, contributed more than anyone to the fact that the Campus sustained minimal damage during the 60's in contrast with other universities around the country. Ernie was a farm boy with hay in his hair who worked his way through school managing cooperative student housing. He had a knack for talking to students and averting or lessening a crisis.

At least a dozen chic women's apparel shops once thrived on the Avenue. If you bought it on the Ave it was something to brag about. In the late sixties their owners sought retirement.

More in keeping with the times, a young woman operated an off-beat boutique just off the Ave. She was about nineteen, tough and, I always thought, beautiful. I am not sure she would appreciate a credit line. In any event, one day a thug showed up across the counter making demands. In the melee she grabbed him in the crotch and with a firm hold and an occasional twitch prepared him to welcome the police.

The Associated Students of the University of Washington (ASUW), led by various presidents, was an essential element of life on the Ave.

Thom Gunn, elected president in 1968, was short and brassy with a mischievous mind. For many students I suspect he represented a welcome return to the zoot suited, ukulele playing, Joe College days of their grandparents. Thom celebrated his election by importing a dancer from California who disrupted the campus by dancing nude in the Quad. The story is that President Odegaard ordered the scandalous display of human flesh stopped. The problem was, all the University administration *staff members* were in the audience.

After the first riots Thom came up with a prescription to cure all animosities, the famous "Love U." It was a Barnum & Bailey approach that found at least one of the banks putting its records in its deepest vault and the Marine Recruiting office removing its files from the District. Thom proved to be dangerous but lots of fun.

Steve Boyd, president in 1969-70, had a childlike face that encouraged trust, and an almost religious faith in his fellow men and women as he feverishly pursued the goal of togetherness. Without his help and the financial support of the ASUW and its members, our shelter—the University District Center (UDC)—would never have existed.

Rick Silverman, a graduate student who served in 1970-71, was a return to the more liberal side. I considered him anti-business and met him only a few times. He served at a difficult period and I would be reluctant to criticize his performance. Rick fathered a Community

Action Conference financed by the ASUW, that focused on the mechanics of community organization. Nationally-recognized participants were brought in from around the country, including a leading conservative.I was most impressed by learning how a few persons could with an imposing letter head, good lungs, and the ability to summon a few troops to storm city hall, impose their will on a City.

The University of Washington branch of Students for a Democratic Society (SDS), a national organization, was a strident, somewhat amorphous group. Its Weatherman faction and other splinter groups were belligerent, dangerous, and given to rock throwing and vandalism. It had overtones of what most of us regard as a desire to overthrow the government, but its principal thrust was against the Viet Nam war. Its effectiveness was blunted when, as I will recount, it seized the Placement Office in Lowe Hall on campus. Whether its members had anything to do with a number of arson fires on campus and the bombing of two University jeeps, was never established. I once helped them find a place to hold a mass meeting, not out of sympathy but to cool their animosity.

The Free University, largely under the guidance of Miriam Rader, the daughter of a liberal professor, was heavily into reforming our society. It held forth on an upper floor in the 4100 block of the Ave. It supported radical causes but was in essence an educational institution with interesting classes, often slanted to the far left, ranging from Karl Marx to photography. I rather admired their approach if not their goals, and I took a photography class.

The church and campus Youth Ministers played an important role in decision making and in binding up wounds. They were key to establishing the University District Center. Because of his direct involvement with students, Dave Royer, the Campus Christian Minister, was perhaps the most active and helpful since he could devote his efforts to community projects such as the University District Center. The church Youth Ministers were important but less visible since the major churches such as University Christian, University Presbyterian, University Methodist, and Congregational had their own "reach out" programs. The youth ministers were all younger than I and perhaps more enthusiastic. When I see them now I realize what a fragile thing is youth.

The University District Center opened in a University Ave building in January 1970. It carried on a host of activities such as counseling but primarily provided shelter (in other locations) for transient young people. It was the creation of a few business persons, the ASUW, hippies and street people, liberals such as Walt Crowley, and the churches. The Center disappointed some because it did not welcome drug users. After months of uncertainty and wrangling over goals it finally zeroed in on serving essentially normal young people, both local and the thousands wandering the country. Many were well educated or at least well informed. Most had a sincere but puzzled concern about the course the world seemed to be taking, particularly in Viet Nam. Many were trying to determine whether their conscience demanded that they flee to Canada.

I can recall a conversation with one of them while we stood over adjoining public urinals. A skinny red-head, he looked hungry. He had drifted to Seattle from the Middle West.

"I just got in town. Do you know any place I could spend the night?" I did — the Center would find him a bed.

I was flattered when another lad we knew as Brare, who had black stubs for teeth and who cut a half moon in the Center's toilet door, came by the office. It was our last meeting and he came to grin broadly and show me his new false teeth. He recently left a phone number but it was incorrect.

Much of our shelter activity centered around the University Baptist Church where George Lawson, the pastor, and the congregation made room in the basement for a shelter.

One source of disruption on the University of Washington campus was the Black Student Union and its supporters. University officials were terrified in February, 1970 when the Union first demanded that the University cancel its sports contract with Brigham Young University. The contract had two years yet to run. Because the Mormons refused to admit Blacks to the priesthood, the students and their supporters argued that it should be cancelled forthwith.

Another source of disruption was SDS (Students for a Democratic Society). Periodically, the Student Placement Office in Lowe Hall invited recruiters offering careers to graduates to conduct business in that office. In April 1969 these included not only corporations such as Weyerhauser but also military recruiters. SDS mounted a protest the goal of which was to block military recruiters by seizing Loew Hall.

Weyerhauser cancelled its interviews on the ground that it did not want to become "pawns in publicity stunts." On 24 April more than 1000 objectors were threatening to occupy the building. Ultimately a few demonstrators succeeded in entering it briefly. Perhaps another 500 students rallied in opposition to SDS. The university administration was baffled. It could hardly call in the Tactical Squad to cart its students off to jail with broken heads. Even while the University was wringing its collective hands a miracle was about to be performed.

The crowd was not unfriendly. Ernie Conrad, a University Vice President and the Attorney General's representative on Campus mingled freely, not realizing that the proceeding was about to come to a "humming" halt that Gilbert & Sullivan would have loved.

No one noticed the pickup truck with eastern Washington plates, piled high with boxes as it edged its way into the demonstrators. Perhaps the driver who hailed from the Yakima Valley feared the crowd and injudiciously hit the throttle. In any event two bee hives fell into the roadway. He later claimed that after the hives fell off demonstrators had broken his windows and damaged the truck. Angry bees buzzed everywhere. The Attorney General was stung but not the Vice President. Demonstrators, both pro and con, fled slapping at bees. Twenty two persons were treated for severe bee stings. The truck driver claimed to be looking for the entomology department. He escaped without a sting by either bees or the police.

Members of SDS continued a more subdued attack on Loew Hall. They overcame the fact that an almost equal number of opponents sought to block their entry. By three o'clock in the afternoon SDS controlled the building. This lasted for half an hour. When they heard a rumor that the police had been called, they vacated. The Loew Hall incident was over. The University temporarily suspended several students including Robbie Stern for this action and for an earlier one involving a United Fruit Company recruiter.

During the fifties and early sixties businesses on the Ave had flourished. Homecoming festivities meant bonfires on Fraternity Row and decorations along the Ave. The World's Fair in 1962 was an exciting time, also a turning point. The new Space Needle looked down on a Coney Island of the Pacific Northwest. Overhead, gondolas spanned the Fair. A multi colored fountain danced to a musical accompaniment. There were dozens of rides including a roller coaster, and a long row of toss-the-bean-bag-into-the-ring type carnival games. The exhibits of many countries—Mexico's was perhaps the most colorful—were almost lost in a sea of entrepreneurial frenzy. All was connected to downtown by an elevated monorail that still runs today.

The Fair was flamboyant and raucous. Gracie Hansen's chorus line came closest to a display of female flesh. One story has it that a grandson, thinking to shock his grandfather, took him to see Gracie's show after which the following exchange took place.

"Gramps, how'd you like it?"

"Not much. Never did cotton to spectator sports."

Perhaps inspired by the Fair, coffee houses opened on the Avenue. Peg and I found them delightful. If the haze in some was in fact marijuana smoke we never suspected.

Among the coffee houses Cafe Encore was our favorite, Its owner Robert Bernard Shaw, a plump, talkative former musician, and the Encore itself, each have a story to tell.

I recently visited his antiques store. His red hair that had earned him the nickname "Rusty" had turned thin and off-white, his paunch had expanded, but his spirits had not flagged. As we talked he squirmed in his chair.

"I've got to have a cigarette."

"Go ahead.

"It's the damn fire department. They came by a couple of days ago with a nine-man, two million dollar rig and told me they'd cite me the next time they found me smoking in the store."

The store has a dutch door. With the lower half closed we continued our conversation with me on the inside, Shaw on the outside.

After Shaw was discharged from the service following World War II, he spent five years playing jazz organ, booking into supper clubs and saloons around the country. During that time he collected whatever caught his fancy, including antiques. He shipped them to friends who stored them in basements and attics. When he retired from the club circuit he returned to Buffalo to open an antiques store. This lasted for three years until a bank bought out his lease in exchange for financing a three month trip to Europe.

Back in the United States, he began a tour in search of a spot to fulfill a dream. Europe had convinced him to start a coffee house. He ended up in the University District with 11 dollars. An eager and sympathetic real estate broker rented him the Encore location for 50 dollars a month with the first month's rent payable in sixty days.

In 1956 the Encore, with thirteen small tables, a tiny spot for a performer, and limited food service, was off and running long before the first month's rent was due. At first a fancy pastry and coffee cost only 50 cents. Over the years it rose to three dollars. The performers survived on tips. After the first week customers were being turned away. Players such as the guitarist Willy Younger felt proud to appear at the Encore.

The Encore policy was, to put it tritely, "good, clean fun." No drugs, no off color jokes. The kind of place you could safely go with your maiden aunt.

Disaster struck in 1964. Shaw had already bounced a number of belligerent marijuana users. When hardcore drugs began to appear, he closed the Encore forever. A short time later two mothers of Lakeside school students brought him a cake and expressed their appreciation for the way the Encore had met the needs of their children.

I asked Shaw, "Would you like to do it again?"

"If this were 1956 and not the scene in 1994 the answer would be yes. It was a devil of a lot of fun."

Pamir house on the lower Ave was popular for its sentimental ballads. One not so sentimental ballad dwelt on the slaying of an unfortunate mistress whose presumed sole remains consisted of an unidentifiable ear the police found in the septic tank. In 1965 the Pamir House was replaced by a Christian Science reading room.

The Eigerwand Coffee House across from the Pamir provided discussion, debate, and kindred spirits. These plus the Century tavern at the north end of the Avenue near the Encore and famous for its selection of beer and camaraderie, the Blue Moon off the Ave on N.E. 45th and, of course Wiseman's, accounted for most of the night life in the District. But the Coffee Houses were not long in passing from the scene as drugs and drug busts became more common. Peg and I had listened as the virtues and dangers of marijuana were debated, particularly at the Eigerwand.

The Eiger, where we often spent a pleasant hour, evolved into a spot where smack and LSD were peddled. It was being operated as a coffee house but breaking all the rules in violation of both the lease and the law. I am sure the owner did his best to control the situation without success.

Peg's stepnephew, Gordy, a lad I barely knew, frequented the Ave. A sallow lad in his teens he probably enjoyed the popularity he attained by listening to his peers describe the merits of drugs, particularly LSD. Whether he sampled its claimed magic before taking an overdose, presumably with his pals at the Eiger, is not clear.

Gordy was no angel. Nevertheless, LSD convinced him that he could fly. I have often gruesomely wondered if he flapped his arms as he sailed off the University bridge and hit the shore below.

Enough was enough. Gordy's death prompted us to buy the building for 1000 dollars down. We gave the Eiger's owner a choice. Either operate the Eiger as a true coffee house in compliance with the law and their lease or be thrown out. He at first refused. We began a law suit and he vacated the premises in May, 1967. We promptly leased them for less rent to a Japanese grocer whose friendship we still enjoy.

Even before the Eiger closed, many were arguing that Berkeley and its Telegraph Avenue were forecasting our future. I began to make sporadic trips to that city. The possibility was real.

I watched Telegraph Avenue in Berkeley become a street of iron grills and boarded windows. Some merchants waited for their leases to run out before moving to Shattuck. Others simply gave up.

In Berkeley I talked to young people on the street about drugs, about their dislike of the police and of the establishment. Just as we found later in Seattle, many were anarchists who argued that the masses would always produce a leader.

"Aren't you concerned about who will run the country?"

"Hell no! Someone will always be there to take over."

Few were students, although students no doubt showed up for marches, riots, and possibly for their drug supply.

I had trouble explaining my adverse stand on marijuana. I was convinced, more than ever, that it kills a younger user's learning initiative. But was it worse than booze? I began to have doubts. As I watched Berkeley I become increasingly fearful of what harder drugs and an increasingly transient population might do to our own Avenue as we progressed further into the sixties. Until later in the decade there seemed little outcry in Seattle about Viet Nam. In March, 1967 *Seattle Magazine* reviewed the situation and concluded that "[t]he most singular fact about the local peace groups is not their zeal but their astonishingly small number of active participants—probably not more than 500." In contrast to East Coast schools where the war issue predominated, in Seattle drugs, police harassment, and civil rights played a greater role at least until May, 1970 when Ohio National Guardsmen at Kent State shot into an antiwar demonstration and killed four students.

In Berkeley, as in Seattle, some people were extolling LSD as the panacea for our woes. "Tune in-drop out." In Seattle zombies who overdosed back then still walk the streets in the University District. Some professors echoed Timothy Leary in shouting its virtues. Some may still be doing so today, hopefully detached from a teaching position.

Monty West, our local LSD guru, a fiery exponent of a purposeless world, will appear only this once. I thoroughly disliked him. *Seattle Magazine* summed up his philosophy in June 1967. "There are no straight kids anymore. They're either hippies or they've got so many hang ups they can't think straight. They've taken a good look at the adult phoney world and don't want any part of it." At a church gathering I once debated the drug culture with him. His favorite audience jaw dropping phrase was, "Everything's all fucked up!"

It was heroin (smack), then cocaine and speed that hit us the hardest. By 1965 a network of dealers had made the district their headquarters. It was often difficult to negotiate one's way down the sidewalk through the buyers, sellers, and hangers on. If you were young you might be offered drugs half a dozen times while walking one block. It was said that the manager of Penneys spent as much time chasing needle users out of the rest rooms as he did merchandising.

The Open Door Clinic on Roosevelt Way did all it could with meager public and city support to treat with methadone and counseling the victims of the drug revolution. Finally, depleted of both funds and enthusiasm, the Open Door closed. Its principal founder and operator, Lee Kirschner, deserves more credit than she will ever receive.

The pressures on merchants were severe. For many of them, but not for the head shops, business had gone to hell.

We begged for police but their officious approach and their us-versus-them attitude that many continue to harbor even today embarrassed the more liberal business owners and unnecessarily antagonized the pushers, the street crowd, and many students. The antagonism of one policeman, a John Birchite, was particularly galling. Perhaps certain police officers overused their clubs dealing out whacks and prods with orders to move on. Jan Tissot organized a watch dog operation to prowl the Avenue and register complaints. Many businessmen realized that the police were often overbearing, but what can you do when someone is out to wreck the system that keeps you alive? They also regarded Jan as an anarchist.

I must concede that the police took about as much abuse as anyone, except a Joan of Arc, could stand. But they often overreacted, especially the few with John Birchite tendencies. I suspect that police-escorted visits into the alley were not uncommon.

Many of the older officers, I am sure, remembered the days when if you swore at a policeman you were inciting a breach of the peace on his part and it was off to the poky.

Were it not for the recent improvement in police relations my own experiences, one of which I will shortly recount, might have lead me to agree with Jan's concern.

Our first hint of real trouble on the Avenue as well as a glimpse into the future was provided by the University District Movement (UDM) in 1967.

Chapter 5

University District Movement

Perhaps it is because there is no penalty for losing that radical groups can scare the daylights out of the establishment. The University District Movement (UDM) emerged in 1967 and consisted of a few vocal leaders supported by the underground paper, *The Helix*, as well as by hippies and students recruited at campus rallies. It became a short opening skirmish in what was to become a long period of unrest.

If an alien spacecraft had landed on the Ave, merchants, bankers, and Cal McCune could hardly have been more surprised. Out of the blue the UDM blasted us with accusations: students were overcharged, the Chamber of Commerce was urging restaurants to deny service to "Fringies," the merchants supported the police, and the fuzz were being brutal (probably true). In sum it was a concoction with little truth, false conclusions, and lies with little if any justification. We wondered why? It took the business community too long to find out. Perhaps we never did.

Cal McCune at a 1967 meeting. Photo by Alan Lande.

In retrospect, at least in my opinion, the scenario is easy to unravel. Without knowing the hidden agenda we were baffled.

The Id and the Bookworm occupied adjoining storefronts off the Ave on 42nd N.E. They both specialized in counterculture activities. The Id tended to be more arty. Its owner, Steve Herold, made the mistake of offering for sale a book containing photographs of the sexier temple art of India. He was convicted of dealing in pornography. He appealed and the court found that the book had at least some artistic merit. His attorney was William L. Dwyer, now a Federal District Court judge. The landlord relented. The Id continued in business for several years.

The Chamber of Commerce was unaware that the landlord of the Bookworm and the Id had given both a notice to vacate. It therefore felt particularly put upon by the UDM's claims of wrongdoing. The UDM's attack was engineered by a group of casting directors consisting primarily of the underground newspaper *The Helix*, Walt Crowley, Robbie Stern, Suzi Stern and the Delays. Together they designed a scenario calculated to turn the Ave upside down.

The Chamber invited UDM leaders to attend their weekly meeting at the Sheraton Motor Inn. Robbie Stern took over the meeting. From the podium he shouted accusations against the merchants that his supporters echoed. The Chamber members responded in kind. Tempers flared. Our regular speaker on an unrelated subject never reached the podium. Instead, Robbie Stern harangued us about our sins. We left the meeting befuddled. They stayed behind and held a vitriolic news conference. Did they really feel that we had done all the things of which they accused us? What in heavens name was their real objective? That afternoon Miles Blankenship, the president of the Chamber, issued a statement hotly denying the claims of the UDM. Possibly they thought that if our feet were held to the fire we would intuitively sense and deal with, not the claimed abuse of students and the crowd on the street, but their less self righteous true goal. Not until after a late night session in my office did I have an inkling as to their true intent. My impression even then was that they were trying to save the Id and the Bookworm. Walt disagrees. He advises that the Bookworm was reconciled to moving, that the issue was the Id. Walt may be right.

The Bookworm may have hoped for a reprieve, but on 12 March 1968 the Delays announced that, in combination with a group known as the Brothers, they were looking for a new location. The Brothers claimed to be a religious organization dedicated "to ideals of true individual freedom." Some of its supporters, including Walt Crowley and Paul Dorpat, were ordained for two dollars by a California organization called "The Universal Life Church." Protected by the separation of church and state I doubt if its authenticity was ever questioned. When I later became acquainted with Walt Crowley he rather jestingly still carried the card ordaining him to perform religious rites and ceremonies including marriages, which he had done, by his count, at least ten times.

A group of law school professors joined the fray. They decried the failure to recognize differences in dress and behavior but aimed their principle criticism at the School Board and City Council which had refused to provide speaking platforms to the psychedelic drug exponent Timothy Leary and to Stokely Carmichael, a black leader who later became a voice for moderation. They argued that democracy is ruled by a "confidence in the prevalence of reason...the belief that people will on the whole and in the long run choose the good and reject the bad. If this confidence is lacking, free institutions cannot function." Whether the professors' conclusion is being borne out by history could be another subject for debate.

With my own usual confidence that anything can be talked or argued out, I arranged an evening meeting in my office with UDM leader Robbie Stern and two of his associates. It was my first personal encounter with the so-called "radicals." We didn't understand each other and I played the wrong cards. Perhaps they did too.

I led off by attacking the falsity of their charges and it immediately turned into an unimportant argument. Robbie made one remark which in retrospect I realize should have been the clue to a solution. The gist of it was that there wasn't time to do anything else.

Soon everyone's hair stood on end. By the time it dawned on me that their purpose was probably to save either the Id and Bookworm or both from being evicted we had gone beyond rational discussion.

The merchants, few of whom had ever heard of the Id and Bookworm, were infuriated by the ruckus and concluded that the two stores contained a nest of marijuana smoking communists if not down-right anarchists reading and distributing subversive literature. By revealing my sympathy with the merchants I lost the initiative. The radicals frigidly departed. If I felt a pain in my rear it was because I was mentally kicking myself.

I probably could have pulled strings and killed the eviction. I wish I had. The landlord relented with respect to the Id after the Courts exonerated Steve Herold. By 17 April the Brothers and the Bookworm were in the process of moving. Both faded away soon after they moved to 5824 Roosevelt Way.

The UDM withered away also, but its spirit would be reincarnated a short time later under other names and other causes.

My next effort at diplomacy was more successful. John Mitsules, my closest ally, arranged it. According to John the beat cops were making life miserable for Black Panthers soliciting funds for their breakfast program. John invited the Panthers to meet with me and the patrolmen in my office. By design the two blacks came in first. Elmer Dixon, a handsome, well known member of the Black Panthers, was to act as spokesman. He proved to be intense but easy to talk to. I liked him immediately. When the two cops showed up we kept it cool.

Elmer quoted the cops' demands:

"Back against the wall!"

"Holding out your container is O.K."

"Approach anyone and you'll get busted!"

In addition the cops deliberately slurred the name of Elmer's companion, a likeable pre-med student.

The obviously unfriendly officers said nothing to contradict Elmer Dixon. We ended up agreeing that solicitation was O.K. "Just don't impede pedestrians."

For two Christmases after that I took a five pound box of chocolates to the Black Panther office in Madrona. I refused to identify myself. Perhaps I was unconsciously trying to plant a seed of understanding.

With such an attitude I am puzzled why, at a later date, I should attempt to run down a black looter with my car. My answer, at least to myself: since childhood I have regarded a person's possessions as often all that he has achieved from a lifetime of struggle. These are more important than the life of a looter. At Halloween I might have helped put the cow on top of the Rivoli Theater's roof, but I never destroyed someone's property. Perhaps the closest I came was the night two buddies and I invaded Washelli Cemetery. It had a huge sign "WASHELLI" on a hill above the Cemetery with the letters formed by incandescent bulbs. Our goal was to unscrew all the lights but HELL. Fortunately we were nabbed on the way up the hill rather than on the way down. We pled a midnight stroll.

After the UDM, tensions on the Avenue continued to tighten. Drugs and their use proliferated, and the police and the hippies virtually went to war. On 14 August 1969, a few days after the police broke

up a giant beer bust at Alki in West Seattle, the lid blew off. It was my first experience with tear gas and it made me realize that, aroused to do battle, I too could lose control and, regardless of consequences, become as dangerous as any rioter. A heady feeling I must admit.

Meeting of various factions. Photo by Alan Lande.

Following the UDM upheaval, participants from all sides began a series of public meetings. For those of us with a touch of ego or a desire to wave a flag, whether blood red or red, white & blue, it was a great opportunity. The object was to achieve a working relationship between the "fringies" (a word coined by Lillian Beloin, editor of the *University District Herald*), the business community, students, and most difficult of all, the police.

We began meeting in September 1967. In the broadest sense the meetings represented an effort to achieve brotherly love and understanding. They were chaired by a liberal professor, John Chambless, and sponsored by the University, the YMCA, and the YWCA. They provided a forum for each of us to exercise his or her right to free speech, but little else was accomplished. The UDM was dying, if not dead. The Bookworm had moved to a new location. Steve Harold appeared to be winning his pornography case and his landlord had relented. Saving the Id, which continued to operate for several years, had apparently become the sole objective of the UDM. If so the UDM could retire with as much dignity as its tactics would permit. The meetings soon followed the UDM into the grave.

The best that can be said is that all parties were somewhat chastened and we at least tried to get along. While little love was generated, at least many of us now knew each other on a first name basis. Later this proved helpful when, after the 1969 riots, we again sat down and more earnestly tried to mutually bandage our bloodied heads.

In 1969 the issues centered on law enforcement and claims of police harassment, the use and sale of drugs, and the behavior of both merchants and street people.

We began meeting on 11 September 1969 in the Student Union Building after the August riots and continued into mid-October. I attended all but the last two meetings realizing as I did that the pounding in my veins was probably high blood pressure. Then one evening a creepy cuss I always thought was a prime pusher remarked that I belonged in retirement in Sun City. If I had quickly responded, "And you should be in jail," I might have cooled off.

On the following day, after I explained to my doctor what I was doing, he took my blood pressure three times and assured me that unless I had suicide in mind I should "cut out that nonsense."

Given this excuse I here rely mainly on newspaper accounts rather than on what might, in any event, prove to be a faulty memory. Primarily I follow reporter Mike Wyne's accounts in the Seattle *Times* and those of Bruce Johanson, a bit of a radical, in the *Daily*.

At the first meeting on 11 September sparks immediately began to fly. The Street Caucus, a group of perhaps twelve hippies headed by Jan Tissot, played a twenty minute tape of recorded examples of police harassment. Some, such as officious orders to "get off the street," hit the mark; others were simply an officer, probably battered by verbal abuse, losing his temper. One officer was recorded ordering a woman to wear a brassiere—no credit to the police.

Walt Crowley commented that historically the police had sought to make it difficult for hippies to remain on the street. Inwardly the merchants present must have said "Great work." Walt continued, "We are dealing with tactics, not individuals." The police responded that the majority of Seattle's arrests for narcotics, AWOL from the military, and child runaways were made in the University District.

(The Washington Legislature's current view of civil rights may assist in eliminating runaways from the list.)

The participants finally agreed to draft a code providing standards for street civil rights and courtesy. The work would be undertaken by a group of five including merchants, police, students, street people, and independents. The merchants chose Andy Shiga to represent them. Future public meetings were to center primarily around the proposal they drafted.

At subsequent meetings Jan Tissot, leader of the University Street Caucus, occupied center stage. He was closely followed by the police, a few self-interested drug dealers, Seattle Deputy Mayor Ed Devine, students, and business representatives, all running in confused circles. Walt Crowley stood in the wings. The language of the Code of Conduct, initially pretty much hatched and drafted in the *Helix* office by the group comprising one representative of each faction was, I am sure, primarily his handiwork.

This initial effort fell apart as the police and the Street Caucus fought over language relating to detainment for inquiry before arrest. It was finally agreed that each side would set forth its position. Instead, ten street people — led by Jan Tissot — walked out. Correctly or not, this was taken as tacit approval. On 13 October the somewhat leaky Code of Avenue Behavior was adopted. This, plus the transfer of two over-zealous policemen, served to maintain a semblance of

University District riot, 1969. Photo by Alan Lande.

peace on the Ave until the 1970 shootings at Kent State when, across the country and in Seattle, hell broke loose.

The Code of Avenue Behavior was in place, but no one jumped for joy.

A beat cop quipped, "The Courts change laws like socks."

Walt Crowley commented, "We're not writing a statement, we're writing a serial."

Capt. Mel Matheson, police community relations director, read a petition signed by 1500 citizens denouncing the invasion of the District by "dregs of society."

There was little humor expressed at the meetings except by accident. Typical was the tension-relieving announcement by Jan Tissot that his job required him to leave the meeting early.

"What are you doing Jan?"

"Checking I.D. at the Blue Moon."

Times reporter Mike Wyne, after a meeting on 19 September summed up the situation rather well. He wrote that Officer Robert Whalen reported that tensions had already eased. "There is a friendliness from persons we stop or say hello to or talk with."

Ted Garfield, a student, urged that police be required to explain each step, such as why they are searching a person for weapons or suspected drugs.

Sgt. Don Grasby responded. "There are a lot of things present in an officer's mind when he makes an arrest. If I have to make a speech, this is silly."

He continued, "I've got a suit, badge that tells you who I am, but I don't know who you are — I've got to be concerned with a lot of things."

Tissot tangled with Officer Falk, a Birchite type who was reported to have developed his own rogues gallery by backing young people against the wall and taking their pictures. Later Tissot and Faulk tried to talk out their differences. Tissot summed up that conversation by remarking, "That's what we want, to get to know you."

"The best way to get to know someone on the street is to share a joint," Tissot told the officers. As an alternative he suggested they might try yoga or Zen-Buddhism. "We want police who want to 'rap' with us and understand us."

No doubt Tissot would share a joint but in my opinion he was far too dedicated to his political agenda to personally participate in hard drug activity.

Tissot called the sale of drugs the major industry in the "hip" community, adding that it was approached in good conscience because members do not feel all drugs are wrong.

"We're seeking to change laws," he said. We are not seeking an open avenues for laws to be broken. We're trying to get by, not trying to make a million selling dope."

In retrospect Jan was most certainly a thorn in the side of the Establishment. Did we deserve it? Probably not as applied to drugs. Certainly our fears and crumbling businesses made it difficult for us to deal realistically in other areas such as human rights and aspirations. Today the drug situation on the Avenue has worsened. But if the merchants, Jan, and the Police sat across a table today I feel that the discussion might be more productive than it was over twenty years ago. For one thing, the merchants would correct their mistake of not taking a tough stand on drugs. They would demand street participation in their elimination as the price of peace.

Chapter 6

Floyd the Flag Burner

I first encountered Floyd Turner early one summer morning. He was clinging, like a four legged spider, to the rock wall of Pay n' Save, his bare toes feeling for crevices as he descended. I watched in surprised fascination as a gaunt young man in his early twenties, with bushy hair, wearing frazzled jeans, reached the sidewalk and slipped on his sandals.

I tried "Nice climbing" for an opener.

"I'm Floyd Turner," he responded somewhat tartly, and walked away.

I last glimpsed Floyd at the University District Street Fair. He was standing barefoot on a cake of ice and hawking Popsicles with a spiel about climbing Mt. Rainier in his bare feet. By this time we had developed a mutually suspicious relationship. I hazarded, "How's it going Floyd?"

Floyd Turner.
Photo by Erik
Lacitis.

"No time to talk," he replied.

In between these two glimpses of Floyd much happened. Particularly Floyd's trial for flag burning which Shakespeare would have turned into a howlingly funny comedy.

Floyd's origin is uncertain. I have been told that two kindly local anarchists, George Crowley and his wife (both now deceased) found him as a waif in his mid-twenties in Idaho or Montana and brought him to Seattle. Floyd himself gave varying accounts of his past and indeed took pleasure in misleading the public, the police, and the courts.

According to George Crowley when they found Floyd he could

not read, could write his name only by block printing, and had a vo-cabulary of about 200 words. They taught him whatever reading and writing skills he possessed.

His mentor, George Crowley. as quoted in the July 1967 issue of *Seattle Magazine* commented, "Floyd can't express his feelings by writ-ing or talking as we do. He has to make some kind of graphic demon-stration."

Floyd sat on no radical councils. He expressed himself best by taking off his clothes. On the other hand he could become unendingly garrulous on the witness stand, to the dismay of his attorney.

The anarchist teachings of the Crowleys may account for some of the fact that Floyd's crusades often ended up in the police booking office.

While Floyd is usually thought of as an alleged flag burner, his frequent court appearances in 1966 in Municipal Court, before Judge Charles Z. Smith are equally interesting.

Judge Smith is a black jurist, later to serve on the State Supreme Court. Floyd made many appearances before Judge Smith who prob-ably took more interest in him than did anyone except the Crowleys. Floyd's first appearance before the judge resulted from his staging a one man sitdown in the revolving door of a doughnut shop. Floyd, who is white, told the judge it was because the shop discriminated against blacks. His only witness, a black woman, testified that she had eaten there four years earlier, and had gotten the feeling she was not wanted. The judge ordered, "One day suspended."

Later Floyd was charged with waving a Viet Cong flag at a group of sailors. Later still he set off a fire cracker at a Nazi rally. In each case, "One day suspended."

Floyd's next brush with the law was more serious. He was charged with carrying a concealed weapon. He had responded to an incident in which an allegedly intoxicated off duty policeman had shot a black man in a Chinese restaurant. Floyd purchased a revolver and pro-ceeded to reenact his version of the event by entering the restaurant waving the pistol and giving his imitation of a drunken policeman.

It was too much for Judge Smith, He packed Floyd off to Harborview Hospital for a psychiatric examination. "No mental ill-ness," was the report.

Floyd and the judge finally agreed that if Floyd would take a farm job out of the state the charges would be dropped. He left but soon returned to Seattle, if not on track, at least his old self.

Before describing Floyd's three hour trial for flag burning it is necessary to set the stage and to recount some of the events leading up to one of our police department's finest moments. The entire drama took place at an ancient mansion on Capital Hill then occupied by the Central Area Motivation Program. The date was 12 May 1967. Ten civil rights organizations had rented the premises with a lofty purpose in mind. They wished to honor four lawyers who had handled their cases without charge. They threw a party and invited Seattlites of every political persuasion and degree of radicalism.

One staunch Democrat later said, "It was the damnedest party I ever saw. Even the Republicans were nice."

At the trial the witnesses could agree on only one thing. Someone had torched a tiny American flag.

The flag burning appears not to have been on the program. The high point of the evening was to have been smashing a piano on the front lawn with hammers, axes, and crow bars. The significance of this was never revealed. That those attending appreciated music is beyond question. All evening the proceedings were enlivened by a light show and a rock 'n' roll band named Clockwork Orange. It was noise complaints from the neighbors that first brought the police.

We can now take the case to Court. It came to trial on 2 July 1967 in Seattle Municipal Court. Judge Manolides who tried Floyd as a flag burner turned out to be less relaxed and considerably less understanding than Judge Smith. In contrast, the thrust of the defense testimony might be characterized as, "Let's have fun with the Judge." Attorney for the defense was Edmund J. Wood, a liberal, not radical attorney who enjoyed defending the underdog. Perhaps "exasperated" would be the best way to describe Judge Manolides state of mind.

The evidentiary questions alone would have done more justice to a Congressional Investigation than to a three hour trial.

Was Floyd holding the flag or was he the one who lighted it? Did Floyd have anything at all to do with the flag? Was Floyd even present when the flag burned? Can you believe an Anarchist? Was the piano demolished before or after the flag burning?

Either there were many faulty memories or enough perjurers to fill a large jail cell.

Perhaps the most unbiased witness was Louis C. Scott, a black apartment manager. With a pair of powerful binoculars he watched the proceedings from his apartment across the street. At 10:49 o'clock he had called the police complaining of the racket created by Clockwork Orange.

While waiting for the police to arrive, he testified, he witnessed the destruction of the piano. After that, he testified, Floyd appeared and was running around with a small American flag. He stated that while Floyd held the flag, a second man, whose face he couldn't see, burned it with a cigarette lighter.

The first policemen to arrive examined the premises but made no arrests and eventually retreated to the sidewalk across the street. Not until Chief Ramon showed up at 11:30 was Floyd arrested and the partygoers told to cool it, which they did.

The prosecution called four policemen and a TV news cameraman who testified that they heard Turner admit to the burning at a demonstration against police brutality a week later. Apparently fearing that his testimony or demeanor would prove a liability , the defense did not call Floyd to the stand.

At this point the circus began. Floyd's attorney called five witnesses who testified that they did not see Floyd with the flag or hear him state that he intended to burn it. A dusky man, they said, was seen carrying the empty flag staff. Contradicting the testimony of the apartment manager, they insisted the piano was destroyed after the flag burning and not before.

This paved the way for a sculptor, Richard Beyer, to testify that he and Floyd were in a truck picking up the piano at the time the flag burning took place.

After the trial Beyer said that he felt he hadn't helped the situation when he told the police that the party was to thank some lawyers for protecting them against police harassment. At the same time Clockwork Orange was belting out one of its favorite songs:

There's a man with a gun over there
Telling you you've got to beware.
You've got to stop, hey!
What's that sound?
Everybody look what's going down.

The principal witness for the defense, Stan Iverson, was then called. Stan, as we all knew him, was an anarchist who had given up on the Communist Party because of its civil rights record. Iverson swore on oath that it was he who burned the flag, lighting it with matches while an unknown, light haired man, presumably not Floyd, held it. The dark skinned man, presumably not Floyd, had merely stood by and watched. Asked why he burned the flag, Iverson responded: "The flag is associated with militarism, extreme national chauvinism and is used in attempts to bludgeon the people into a sort of monolithic unity."

The judge then asked if he felt his anarchistic beliefs relieved him from telling the truth?

Iverson responded that he had a moral obligation to tell the truth.

Upon further questioning, Iverson conceded that under some circumstances it was permissible to tell lies, but never about important matters.

Judge Manolides obviously put little credence in the defense testimony. He sentenced Floyd to six months in jail and a 500 dollar fine.

Floyd's case was appealed to the Superior Court where another sympathetic and experienced trial attorney, Philip Burton, took over the defense. Burton, of course, hoped for a determination that burning the flag was protected as free speech. It was not to be, but the case was sent back to Municipal Court for a new trial. This time the trial went to a jury. The testimony was much the same except that Floyd took the stand. His account of his relationship with the Doukhabors, a religious sect in British Columbia that burned down their own houses and paraded in the nude, plus his general attitude and police record probably did not help. The jury found him guilty. Once again, "Six months and 500 dollars." The case was appealed to the Supreme Court which heard it *en bank*.

The trial court had given the following instruction: "You are instructed that it is not required that you find that the defendant intended to violate the law. You are only required to find that the defendant performed the physical act charged."

The Court then proceeded to duck the free speech issue and zeroed in on the language of the instruction. The Court's analysis involved a complex review of the history of flag desecration laws in Germany from the time of the Kaiser to date. It concluded that under the Washington statute the defense should have been allowed to "show the jury that," under the statute, "the holding of an American flag while another set fire to it was done, if done at all, without any intent to degrade, desecrate, defile or cast contempt upon it."

The Supreme Court then reversed and remanded the case. Like an artful politician it ducked the important issue—freedom of speech. Such careful consideration, together with legal technicalities, submitting briefs, arguments, and writing the opinion, required from 15 September 1967, the date of judgment in the trial case, to 3 September 1970, three years later.

Floyd was eventually vindicated. Responding to what it considered to be the rather weak approach of the courts toward desecration of the flag, in 1989 Congress passed the Flag Protection Act. It was to prove fruitless. In United States v. Eichman, a 1990 decision, the United States Supreme Court for all practical purposes gutted the handiwork of Congress. In a split decision it held that the Congressional action flew in the face of the free speech guarantee of the First Amendment. In essence the Court held that flag burning is a mode of expression, unlike obscenity or "fighting words," and enjoys the full protection of the First Amendment. It is doubtful if Floyd could have secured a pardon, but in the end he was arguably the victor.

Floyd spent 45 days in jail before being released on bond. In an interview he claimed he had been abused as a flag burner by fellow inmates and indeed he was finally placed in a separate cell. A deputy sheriff asserted that Floyd brought most of his troubles upon himself. This may be true.

Floyd said in an interview: "I tried to tell the other prisoners that when police arrest them they should take off their clothes. That's what Doukhabors do. I'm a Doukhabor, you know. I went up to Agassiz in British Columbia a while back and joined them. They baptized me and everything."

After the trial Floyd's offenses were minor. For instance, he ran around naked in a public campground to protest an alleged inequity.

I like to think that Floyd's final public act did occur and that he at last earned a gold star.

Accounts differ and some say it never took place. They may be correct. After the deaths at Kent State the campus boiled over as related in another chapter. Marches were organized to follow I-5 and public streets from the District to the Federal Court house. Apparently no one requested a parade permit. Certainly none was granted. On one of the marches dozens of police established a line that blocked passage on I-5. Several thousand screaming and determined young people marched toward them. Searching for an opening, the advance halted perhaps 100 feet from the police line. Some say that a naked Floyd danced onto the scene from the side lines and ran in circles between the possible combatants. Tempers cooled and the march proceeded on less travelled streets. The leaders deny Floyd's participation. I prefer to think that they eschewed such an undignified end to the confrontation. Perhaps in the general pandemonium Floyd went unnoticed. If I find him before this is published I shall if necessary make a correction.

In any event I shall continue to think of Floyd as a "peacemaker." I hope not good enough, like the meek, to inherit the earth.

Someday Floyd's tombstone could carry as an epitaph a portion of an interview he gave to Erik Lacitis, now a columnist on the Seattle *Times*: "People tell me I'm crazy, but that's OK, I don't care. I know I can climb mountains barefoot! No one's done that in the U.S. ever before! No one you know, except me."

BRING THE WAR HOME!

ALL SUMMER LONG THE PIGS HAVE BEEN COMING DOWN ON THE BROTHERS & SISTERS IN GOLDEN GARDENS HASSELING THEM FOR ANY & EVERY POSSIBLE REASON. A WEEK AND A HALF AGO THE PEOPLE SAID FUCK-OFF-STOMPED A PIG'S ASS AND MESSED UP HIS CAR.

IT'S BEEN THE SAME THING AT ALKI IN WEST SEATTLE. LAST SUNDAY THE PEOPLE SAID FUCK-OFF! STONED SOME PIGS AND PIG CARS AND BURNED ONE PIG CAR OUT.

THE SCENE IS THE SAME AT PARK LAKE AND LAKE HICKS. THE PIGS ARE ALSO COMING DOWN HEAVY ON THE BROTHERS AND SISTERS THERE.

MONDAY NIGHT, THE SCENE WAS THE U.DISTRICT WHERE HEAVY PIG OPPRESSION HAS BEEN COMING DOWN FOR OVER A WEEK-TRYING TO CLOSE THE SCENE DOWN. PEOPLE CAME TOGETHER AS BROTHERS AND SISTERS TO FIGHT THE PIGS.

For many years, the Black People in Seattle, Wetts, Detroit, Chicago and all over the country have been coming together and fighting the pigs. Because of what we've learned together in the streets we know that black people who are fighting are also our brothers and sisters. In Viet Nam the people have been rising up for years, fighting together against the U.S. pigs. The people are winning in Viet Nam because their spirit is stronger than the guns of the man. That's where we're at. Grooving on the strength of our brothers and sisters all over this earth. All over this planet it's the same war.
WHY ARE WE GETTING TOGETHER TO FIGHT THE PIGS?
A SMALL NUMBER OF PEOPLE IN THIS COUNTRY HAVE A WHOLE LOT OF POWER AND THEY'RE USING THEIR PIGS AND THEIR ARMY TO KEEP THAT POWER.
ON THE STREET, IN THE GHETTO, AND IN VIET NAM THE PIGS ARE COMING DOWN HARD ON THE PEOPLE, BUT THE PEOPLE ARE COMING TOGETHER AND FIGHTING BACK-BROTHERS AND SISTERS FIGHTING TOGETHER AGAINST THIS MONSTER! IF THE MON-STER IS GOING TO BE DEFEATED, PEOPLE HAVE TO COME TOGETHER.

YOUNG PEOPLE ALL OVER THE WORLD ARE COMING TOGETHER AND FIGHTING THE MON-STER. JUST LIKE THE BLACKS CAME TOGETHER LAST MAY IN THE CENTRAL AREA THE PEOPLE AT ALKI, PARK LAKE, LAKE HICKS, GOLDEN GARDENS, THE AVE AND ALL OVER THE CITY HAVE GOT TO COME TOGETHER JUST LIKE THEY DID LAST SUN-DAY AND MONDAY.
WEDNESDAY NIGHT THE BROTHERS & SISTERS ARE GETTING TOGETHER AGAIN AT 7:30 UP ON HIPPIE HILL (NE 42ND & 15TH NE) LET'S BE THERE. THE TIME HAS COME TO BRING THE WAR HOME! GET IT ON!

'We're looking for people who like to draw'
.... THE COMMUNITY

Chapter 7

The Sky Falls

It was a mad, mad schizophrenic idea. An all night revel destined to give the business community and the University fits and to scare the daylights out of its organizers. It came in 1968 to Thom Gunn, ASUW president, who perhaps sensed the ominous rumbling of conflicts to come.

The Great Love-U would cement relationships between the University, the Community, and the Street. That was the bait Thom dangled before us. We bought it hook, line, and almost sinker. John Mitsules, Andy Shiga and I, a few more liberal business types, together with representatives of the ASUW, a number of street people, and members of the student ministry glued it together. I have always thought that Thom was elected President of the ASUW as a relief from the serious sixties. His sense of the preposterous and his flair for the outrageous had much appeal.

"It will bind us all together," assured Thom, with a cherubic look on his non-angelic face. "The students and hippies will know the business community understands them."

"Sounds like a real riot!" a banker tossed back over his shoulder as he left the meeting.

"Yeah!" mused Mitsules. "How about crowd control?"

"Nothing to it—we'll use the Purple Guard," responded Thom. He explained that the Purple Guard was an arm of the Inter-Fraternity Council that kept order at events on Campus.

"All you have to do is get the City to close the 4500 block from seven until eleven o'clock when we'll move it to Frosh Pond for the

Facsimile of a 1969 flier handed out in the University District which I took to the police department.

rest of the night. Also we'll need about 5000 dollars from the Chamber." Full of confidence, Thom had already pulled the strings to make the arrangements.

No sooner was the event announced than John, Andy, and I were in trouble, primarily with the more staid bankers. "What the hell are you guys doing? Trying to start a riot?"

"Don't worry, it's all under control," we assured them. "Anyway we will have a riot if we don't go ahead now." Somehow we raised Thom's 5000 dollars.

Days before the event, two calamities occurred. Mitsules called the Inter-Fraternity Council. "I'd like to talk to whoever is going to be in charge of the Purple Guard on October 1st." "The what guard?"

Thom had "overstated" the Guard's ability to maintain order. Indeed it appeared not to exist, at least not for controlling off campus riots.

The second calamity was worse and gave us an increasingly ominous feeling. On 18 September someone, never apprehended, torched Clark Hall which housed the Naval ROTC. Damage amounted to more than 85,000 dollars.

John Mitsules took action. To keep order he rounded up a committee consisting of Black Panthers, street people, a few business types, community leaders, and of course those among us such as Andy Shiga who had helped organize the event. We would go out in pairs wearing arm bands.

The Marines cleaned out their files and boarded up their recruiting station. At least one of the banks moved its records to the deepest vault.

At 8:00 p.m. on 1 October 1968 the first of five rock bands began to play on a blocked-off Ave. The last was to arrive at Frosh Pond from California at 5:00 a.m. Dancing and general hi-jinks continued on the Ave until eleven. All went well. The Black Panthers helped by standing guard on the roof of a building overlooking the dance.

At eleven the music stopped. There was a stampede to Frosh Pond on Campus. No broken windows, no burned out trash cans, just a street awash in rubbish.

I headed home but the night was not over. Our house was located a mile from Frosh Pond with our bedroom on the side away from

Campus. At about midnight someone I thought was a neighbor tuned in a rock station with a blast that made sleep impossible. Looking out the window and up the hill I could see no lights on. Then a few blinked. Soon windows were glowing all the way up the north face of Capital Hill. "My God!" I said to Peg, "It's coming from Frosh Pond!"

Back on campus the University telephone exchange was being deluged with irate calls. Ernie Conrad, a University Vice President who had somewhat reluctantly given his blessing to the event, was on campus and desperate.

Ernie searched for and finally found Thom Gunn.

"Thom, you've got to move this into the Hub!"

"No way!"

Ernie practically strong-armed Thom to the University's telephone exchange.

Seating him at a switchboard Ernie demanded, "O.K. you take some of these calls." In a moment Thom looked up. "Ernie, I'll do it just for you."

The lights blinked out on Capital Hill. It was 2:00 a.m.

All was well for a time. Then on the morning of 10 August 1969 we complacently read in the morning *Post-Intelligencer* an account of a riot on the previous night at faraway Alki Point. The participants described it as a subdued beach party. The residents across the street screaming "riot," had deluged 911 with frantic calls. It was held as a "rock concert" under city permit. Actually it was a gigantic beer bust. The police ordered the crowd to break up. Someone overturned a beer keg and others threw rocks and epithets. A prowler car was set on fire. Before it was over both the police booking office and the trauma center at Harborview were busy. The true story of what actually took place was virtually impossible to piece together.

Walt Crowley, who at that time I had not formally met, had written an account of these events in his notebook. This item, rather deviously, came into my possession. I thought his notebook account accurate. On the other hand, his piece published in a local paper a few days later read as if the police had broken up an Easter Sunrise Service in Volunteer Park.

Walt had left his notebook on the counter of a drug store. The pharmacist delivered it to me early in the morning on the second day after the Alki riot. A year or two later I returned it to Walt.

I was at my desk perusing Walt's effort when the receptionist interrupted.

"There's a gentleman here and I think you'd better come out."

The stairs had almost been too much for Charley Jenkins, the pudgy proprietor of the Smoke Shop. He slumped in our maroon leather chair, laboring for breath and more red faced than usual, waving a handbill. Between gasps he blurted, "We've got trouble."

Indeed we did.

The thrust of the handbill was that the "Pigs" were using excessive violence, that the Blacks were oppressed, that commencing at 7.30 that night on Hippie Hill (on campus) retribution would be visited upon the Avenue. The handbill (see appendix for complete text) was, to say the least, inflammatory. It was headlined "BRING THE WAR HOME."

The opening paragraph set the tone:

> All summer long the pigs have been coming down on the brothers and sisters in Golden Gardens hassling for any and every possible reason. A week and a half ago the people said fuck-off; stoned some pigs and pig cars and burned one pig car out. . . Wednesday night the brothers and sisters are getting together. Again at 7:30 up on Hippie Hill (NE 42nd and 15th NE) Let's be there, the time has come to bring the war Home! Get it on!

Within the hour I was standing at the desk of an assistant to the Chief of Police waving the handbill.

"We're going to have a problem in the University District." I tried to look desperate.

She took the handbill, but barely glanced at it.

"We see this sort of thing all the time. You can rest assured that nothing is going to happen. If it does we're fully capable of taking care of it."

"But—?"

"I said we would take care of it." The interview was over. My apprehension increased.

I have been told that after my visit there was much scurrying around at the Police Station. If so, it bore little fruit.

I stopped at Seattle Radio on the way back to the District and purchased a radio that carried the police bands. I plugged it into the cigarette lighter.

The business community held hurried meetings but no plan of action developed. Perhaps it would never happen? But the next morning we found that a trash can had been dragged to the center of the main intersection and set on fire, and others had been upset. Our concern mounted. The police presence however, seemed to have been adequate.

At nine o'clock that night I was driving to a meeting of the Cappers Flying Club in West Seattle. I had the police band radio turned on. It appeared to be a normal night and I relaxed. Then the call came. It was, in effect, "All units stay out of the University District until further notice."

An illegal U turn was never more hastily executed.

I turned into the Ave at N.E. 40th Street and drove north. Ahead noisy crowds of young people, most of high school age, were milling about. Perhaps they were a bit shocked by the blacks who had broken into the Blue Beard, a uni-sex store, and were scattering with arm loads of finery. I happened to be driving an intimidating GMC Suburban automobile that I had purchased by telephone from a hospital bed after I'd been broadsided in a Corvair and broken ten ribs. I saw a looter racing across the street and tried to clip him with the right front fender. Fortunately for both of us he saw me and dodged.

Turning a block west to Brooklyn Avenue I drove north to the 4500 block. Parking, I walked over to the Ave through a mid-block driveway. The crowd was almost festive. Occasionally I would hear the crash and tinkle of a broken window. I watched the crowd and concluded that most felt dismayed when this occurred. Very few of them appeared to be students. I unlocked the door to the stairway of my offices, locked it behind me, climbed the stairs, and in a moment was watching from a front window. Suddenly I heard a crash as glass shattered. In moments blacks were gutting Porter & Jensen Jewelers. Although I would shoot looters I often find it difficult to divorce myself from my belief that given the same background most of us might have done the same.

While this was taking place Warren Porter, the owner of the looted jewelry store, was stranded on Whidbey Island. By the time an employee called him after midnight the ferry had already shut down. He paced the beach until dawn waiting for the morning boat, wondering what bankruptcy would be like. Not until he was surveying the wreckage did he remember that his insurance agent had told him that for a few dollars he could purchase riot insurance. So remote had been the possibility that he couldn't remember whether his answer had been "yes" or "no."

At that moment his agent showed up. Warren was insured.

It was almost ten at night when the police finally arrived and tear gas rolled south down the Ave. The Tactical Squad swept the street.

"Get the hell out of here!" was the order. Disobedience was repaid by a whack with a night stick where it would bruise but not fracture. Finally the crowd began to disburse and at midnight I went home to spend a restless night. It disturbed me that only one or two merchants had shown up to defend their property.

The next morning several of us arrived at the Avenue at dawn. Burned out trash cans, broken and boarded up windows that in some cases had provided access to looters, and littered streets furnished evidence of the violent night. By nine o'clock it was obvious that the merchants were still disorganized. The few who would actively help to stem the riots included: Andy Shiga, the peace advocate; John Mitsules, our Viet Nam hardened tough young Greek; and myself, the law and order guy who couldn't get along with the police.

John's contacts with the riot leaders were sufficient for him to ascertain that the worst was yet to come. John called the Chief of Police and extracted a promise that the police would be out in force. Most merchants thought this sufficient. I was surprised at how few of them were on the street when the next riot began. "Shoot it out at the O.K. corral," was admirable but not to be emulated except by a few.

An hour before sundown I cruised the Avenue. A crowd, mostly young and silent roamed the sidewalks and sat on the grass by the post office. There was an oppressive air of expectancy. The huge crowd on "Hippie Hill" on campus, a block off the Avenue, was frightening. I could sense their tense animosity as I drove by. Unless he was already in jail, I expect the crowd included brawny Jim Emerson. I liked Jim, also his buddy who was a drug addict with a yellowish complexion and who predicted he had not long to live. Jim had earned the right to 30 days jail time when he threw a cop completely over the hood of a car the night the riots started.

Peg and I lived a mile away and we had invited relatives for dinner. I made a quick run home. In half an hour we heard the sirens. Accompanied by Peg, a visiting cousin who was a parole officer from California, his daughter, and a nephew, I drove back to the Ave. They expected a sightseeing trip. They ended up hunkered down in the car in case a rock came flying through a window.

We drove toward the battle ground: flashing lights, the shouts of rioters, bull horns, clouds of tear gas, and the shriek of a disorienting sound device. Tear gas now only a block or two away, was beginning to roll down from the north. Turning south we parked in the 4100 block across the street from La Tienda, a store owned and operated by my daughter Leslie. La Tienda occupied half of a frame building. The other half housed a Marine recruiting station.

The Marines had boarded up their windows. A man was trying to remove the plywood. Would he perhaps torch it along with La Tienda? It was not a calm or brave decision to grab a pipe wrench and head across the street. I had turned into an infuriated Dr. Jekyll. Bellowing, probably obscenities, and waving the wrench I charged my intended victim. He ran, leaving the plywood dangling.

It was my turn to retreat. Rocks were showering like hailstones. Looking north toward the cloud of tear gas I could barely see the throwers in the shadow of an unlit building. Retreat was in order. Unhit and still on a victorious high I reached the van. As I pulled into the street it stalled. Frantically I pumped the accelerator. The engine started and a brick banged into the roof. The dent should have entitled it to a Purple Heart. My passengers wanted to go home. If I showed any reluctance I was faking. It was "Home James, and don't spare the horses."

I wondered "What next?"

Early on Friday morning, 8 August, Roy Nielsen the Chamber President called a meeting of the Chamber Board. We decided on a peace plan. Within an hour we had arranged a meeting in the office of Acting Mayor Floyd Miller. Roy, Dick Coppage, John Mitsules and I attended. The gist of our message "We think everyone is ready for peace. Let us give it a try." The response from the City was mixed.

The Mayor was dubious. Councilman Sam Smith favored calling the National Guard as did assistant Chief of Police Neal Mahoney. He objected that the University did not welcome the Seattle Police on Campus. The Chief of the Campus police assured him that in an emergency they were welcome. Thus mollified, Mahoney somewhat grudgingly withdrew his objection provided the National Guard was notified and ready for an emergency.

Reluctantly our scheme was approved but only with the understanding that the National Guard would be a least alerted and police would be standing by.

Many members of the community met with the street people in the Hub and resolved to restore peace. The Chamber rounded up approximately 80 of its members at the University Tower Hotel. They were enthusiastic and desperate. John Mitsulas then took charge, using the clothing store he managed as his command post.

Before dusk signs were posted on boarded up windows such as "This is a symbol of peace. Do you have the courage to live by it?" Another sign, "We want peace in Viet Nam. Why not peace on the streets of home?"

We paired off wearing white arm bands painted with the peace symbol and began our patrols. My partner was a hippie. The crowd was friendly and seemed to be as pleased as if we had ended a family quarrel.

It was an exhilarating evening that would have disappointed an anarchist but left most of us with a happy memory.

The next morning we totalled our losses from the two previous nights of rioting. At least four stores had been looted. Uncounted windows had been broken, some more than once. Damage at the Pacific National Bank amounted to 25,000 dollars. There had been numerous injuries, none life threatening, and many arrests.

The damage in many college communities had been far worse. All of us, the University, the business community, students, and hippies should have been proud. Not until the shooting at Kent State did we have another riot on the Ave.

Chapter 8

We Play with Matches and High Explosives

Several bombings, an attempted arson, and a fire contributed to the night life of the University District. Two of them, the fire in the University's Naval ROTC building and the bombing of the Administration Building were major and remain unsolved. Another was an attempt to firebomb the Air Force ROTC building. The culprits, Trim and Judith Bissel were caught.

The bombing of the Administration Building occurred at 3:30 a.m. on 29 June 1969. An estimated two boxes of dynamite tore a four foot hole in the reinforced concrete floor at the entrance. A maintenance person in the building was uninjured but damage totalled more than 300,000 dollars and included stained glass windows in the Suzzalo library and shattered windows in other buildings including Parrington Hall and apartments as far away as 15th N.E. There was no advance warning and at the time no group was particularly out of sorts. Speculation ranged from California radicals to perhaps a disgruntled employee. Substantial rewards were offered but no one was ever charged.

The Naval ROTC building caught fire on 19 September 1968. The damage was severe, about 85,000 dollars, but again the culprits could not be identified.

Trim Bissell and his wife Judith attempted to firebomb the Air Force ROTC building on 18 January 1970. The bomb was badly wired and did not go off. They had a history of less serious radical activities. The judge concluded they could safely be released on 25,000 dollars cash bail. His parents put up bail and both promptly disappeared.

They had belonged to a violent group known as the Weathermen. Placing the incendiary device had apparently become a test of their willingness to participate in the group's activities. They split up after skipping out. Judith remained

Jan Tissot, foe, now friend, at a 1969 meeting. Photo by Alan Lande.

active in radical activities. In 1977 she was arrested, tried and served 21 months. Trim settled in Eugene, Oregon after his one serious act of violence and forever altered his life. After passing a high school equivalency test he completed his college education under the name Terry Peter Jackson, received a Masters Degree in physical therapy and was practicing in a Eugene hospital when he was arrested on Tuesday evening 20 January 1987. Extradited to Seattle, Trim entered a plea of guilty to possessing an unregistered destructive device and was sentenced to a term of two years in a minimum security prison in California. Judge Walter McGovern was obviously both deeply touched and troubled when he passed sentence. Judge McGovern observed that he was "morally compelled" to incarcerate Trim (now Terry Jackson) Bissell just as Trim (Terry) had felt he was morally compelled to plant the bomb in an effort to halt the Vietnam war.

The Post Office bombing was short on damage but long on comedy.

The events before the bombing have been reconstructed. This is a possible scenario. It could have started days or weeks before in a dingy University District apartment, possibly in the attic of a dilapidated house whose walls were covered with heroic posters and slogans, as well as sagging wall paper reeking of mold and cigarette smoke tinged with pot.

Four men, Jan Tissot, John Edward Van Veenendal, Michael Stephen Reed, and Jeff Desmond, were in a room speculating how best to dramatize the cause of anarchy. One with long hair and granny glasses, Jan Tissot, wrote romantic poetry. Another, Jeff Desmond had assured them he knew how to obtain explosives.

"Hey man! How about the Post Office?!"

All agreed it was a great idea. They wouldn't blow up the building, just cause enough damage to make a statement.

There was a catch. Jeffrey Paul Desmond was a police informer.

They selected the night of 3 March 1970. That night the pavement glistened under a steady drizzle. Night hawks searching for insects fluttered in the glow of street lamps. Down the block Wiseman's Cafe, a blob of light with two cars parked in front, was living up to its slogan, "Coffee that brings you back."

Four men in dark clothing parked a car on the north side of the Post Office. Jan Tissot got out carrying two sticks of dynamite attached to a two minute fuse and an igniter that could be pulled to light the fuse. Placing the dynamite between the building wall and a small mail truck, he pulled the igniter and ran. An old jalopy was coming up the alley. Too late Jan realized that the car had stopped and that four men were getting out. Jan recognized the inevitable. They were the police.

"Is that a bomb?" the officer apparently in command inquired in a conversational tone.

"It's going off in two minutes," Jan responded.

Almost nonchalantly the officer in command and Jan walked across N.E. 43rd Street. The remaining cops and conspirators hit the street and sidewalk adjacent to the Post Office, as did Jan and the officer in command once they had reached the other side of the street.

The explosion reverberated up and down the Ave jarring even the less sober patrons at Wiseman's who came out to examine the wreckage. Actually the damage was little more than a bruise. One can wonder if this was intended. Or, in the light of what followed, should one consider the probable source of the explosives?

The conspirators were righteously hustled off to jail by the police. Jeff Desmond, the police informer, was almost immediately released and no charges were ever filed against him.

The others were booked and later released. They were again arrested and released on bail on 24 April 1970.

A number of motions were filed on 12 June. The principal motion was for release of the bail. After much wrangling over a period of several months this was denied.

All these procedural histrionics were accompanied by serious negotiations for a plea bargain. It was now increasingly clear to the three conspirators that the box of dynamite had an unofficial stamp of authority. It may have been supplied by Jeff Desmond. Desmond was fascinated by explosives. He had a stump blasting license and was able to purchase explosives.

Nevertheless, the police and probably the F.B.I. apparently felt some responsibility for the fact that it had been used. According to Jan, the conspirators and their attorney without, of course, Jeff Desmond, met with Stan Pitkin, the United States Attorney. He assured them that they would be given immunity for all the dynamite that had come from the tainted box. They, in turn, agreed to plead guilty to aiding and abetting in the manufacture of illegal explosives.

How widely was such informant-supplied dynamite spread around? Was it, for instance, involved in the death of Larry Ward, a recently discharged Vietnam War veteran with a clean record? Ward's attempt to bomb a real estate office in the Central District was also interrupted by the police. Running away, he was shot dead while still carrying dynamite. Once again, an informer was involved, an ex-convict who was parked down the street. The killing was followed by an uproar heard across the country. The inquest jury of two blacks and three whites found by a three to two majority that the killing was done with "criminal intent." Testimony at the inquest made it quite clear that the police thought they were shooting at another black, believed to be involved in other bombings. Only Larry Ward could have explained his reason for being there. Some speculated that fear of such a disclosure might have been the reason for his death. Charles O. Carrol, the Prosecuting Attorney, refused to prosecute the police officers involved. *The Nation* carried an article entitled "Staked Out For Slaughter." The Los Angeles *Times* on 2 May 1971 ran a lengthy story entitled "Killing Nags Consciences in Seattle." Before writing off Larry Ward as just another crazy bomber he at least deserves *in absentia* a word or two in his defense. He is also entitled to have these put him in the most favorable light.

Larry Ward was 21 years old and just out of the army. Presumably he had been taught what armies are for and may have neglected to turn in this knowledge along with his gun. Assume that he meets an informant turned provocateur in a Central Area hangout. A lurid picture is painted, whether true or not, of the injustices heaped upon the black community by a local real estate office. There is absolutely no risk. All he need do is place a stick or two of dynamite against the building and run to the informants car which will be parked down the block. It quickly becomes a question, not of whether he set off the bomb, but of why he would have done so and how much of a sales job was fed into the equation.

On 25 September 1970, the three Post Office bombing defendants were again jailed and an information was filed charging them under an agreed plea — their participation in assembling an explosive device.

All three pled guilty and on 10 November 1970, were sentenced to fifteen months. They entered McNeil Island Penitentiary on 16 November. They had already spent eight months in the King County jail and were released from McNeil after seven months.

The last note in the file shows that the defendant's bail was released to the Conspiracy Defense Fund on 22 November 1970.

What happened to police informer, Jeff Desmond? He is dead. It is a long and somewhat bloody story.

Jeff Desmond, the informant who had participated in the Post Office bombing, was killed on 17 August 1975 in his Seattle apartment on Eastlake Avenue East. Police Chief Robert Hanson said "it has the appearance of a flat-out assassination." Two persons entered Desmond's apartment, and muffling the sound of a small caliber pistol with a pillow, shot him once in the chest. The killers were never identified and the finger pointed in many directions. Least probable were the Post Office bombers. Desmond could do them no further damage.

Almost since childhood Desmond had been fascinated by explosives. He had worked as a stump blaster and was licensed to buy dynamite. Staffers of a Congressional Committee had interrogated him and found him unreliable. They decided not to call him before the Committee. How many other sticks of dynamite he passed out and to whom is unknown. Perhaps to anyone who would give him drugs. Induced by his need for narcotics, who might he have implicated and to what might he have confessed?

Erik Lacitis wrote an article in the Seattle *Times* on 18 August 1975, which carried the headlines: "Out to get me," and "Desmond feared federal agencies." J. Earl Milnes, Special Agent in charge of the Seattle FBI had been quoted at the time of the Post Office bombing in the Seattle *Post-Intelligencer* as saying, "This man was never an informer for the FBI." However, a three part article in the *Post-Intelligencer* in July 1971 claimed "reliable sources confirm that police gave Desmond 500 dollars and that Desmond had some contact with the FBI." Even granting that Desmond was highly unreliable, the newspaper interviews and accounts both in 1971 and after his death leave little doubt that he was justified for any one of several reasons, some undisclosed, in fearing for his life.

Were the Police and probably the FBI at fault? Of course. On the other hand it could be argued that they had little alternative. The government was being undermined by dangerous groups of revolutionaries who would stop at nothing and would like nothing better than to force its collapse. There had been approximately 70 unsolved bombings in the city. Entrapment and letting them hang themselves seemed to the police to be a logical remedy. In fact, there was a question whether it was entrapment. In the course of one of the hearings U. S. District Court Judge William Goodwin noted that the definition of entrapment includes the requirement that the persons entrapped "had no predisposition to commit a crime."

In fact, the nation was itself entrapped in an undeclared war. Soldiers of a foreign power who landed on our shores would promptly be destroyed. In a domestic situation carrying equal peril, our front line troops in the form of the FBI and the police are almost powerless unless civil rights are suspended as was done during the Civil War. Hopefully this may never occur. Perhaps a more modest interpretation of a few constitutional provisions might suffice.

With pleasure I report that all three participants in the Post Office bombing have found important roles in our society and are doing well both for themselves and for us.

In February 1970 the Black Student Union began pressuring for the cancellation of the Brigham Young University athletic contract under the terms of which the University of Washington was obligated to engage in athletic competition with that school. They charged that Mormons did not admit blacks to the priesthood. When the University rebuffed their overtures they repeatedly marched and shouted through bull horns. They invaded six buildings around the Quad but this failed to budge the University's Executive Vice President John Hogness. The students then announced that on 11 and 12 March 1970 they would again march on the Administration Building and sit in until their demands were met.

Negotiations with the leaders of the Black Student Union might have been possible. There was no way, however, that they could have controlled a small group of their more radical members, to say nothing of radical hangers-on, both white and black, from off campus who were dedicated to violence.

Two examples are to be found in the *Daily*. On 3 February the *Daily* carried an editorial written by its editor, Steve Weiner. The thrust of the editorial was that religions often espouse stupid beliefs but this was their right. Egg throwing would not change the religious mind and until a new revelation came along there was nothing to be gained but bad blood. He concluded: "The only thing worse than a person who does all his operating on principles of 'faith' is the person who challenges such a position with equally irrational acts."

The Editor's office was quickly trashed. Weiner was shoved around.

On 12 March 1970 the *Daily* reported that Professor David H. Pinkney was conducting a history class when the demonstrators entered Savery Hall. They marched past the classroom entrance, and a student rose to close the door. The demonstrators forced it open and the Professor told the student to take his seat.

The *Daily* reported:

> Several demonstrators then entered the room and occupied the front of the platform. The class remained quiet in a show of support for Prof. Pinkney, who stopped his lecture when the demonstrators began taunting the class.
>
> Three cans full of garbage were then thrown into the room.
>
> One black demonstrator who was carrying a stick, began shouting racial epithets and obscenities at the class.

A woman student in the class began screaming 'stop it, stop it,' and the noise and confusion grew. Prof. Pinkney then dismissed the class.

As students began leaving, several of the class began harassing the demonstrators. The black man with the stick advanced and struck a white woman on the head yelling, 'I told you to get out of here, bitch.

A student, a white, dared the black to put down his stick. The demonstrator swung the stick twice, knocking the student down and apparently injured him.

All of this was enough for the University. In the face of a threatened full scale attack on 12 March 1970, the University brought in an undisclosed number of plain clothes and Tactical Squad members.

Carl Miller, a black leader, made the following comments to a crowd of 2500 meeting in the Hub: "Anyone who believes that those policemen out there won't kill you is in for a very rude awakening." The BSU "does not intend to get our bodies beaten, that will change nothing." He went on to say that the issue at stake is "racism, pure and simple."

The demonstration was called off. It was in any event the end of the Quarter and the next appearance of the Black Student Union was to be a more temperate one to plead its case before the legislature.

On 27 March President Odegaard made a report to the Board of Regents. He placed the blame not so much on the Black Student Union as on a small group of its members who, together with outside radicals, were in effect revolutionaries who would go to any length to bring down the institutions and to destroy the traditional framework of our society. He made it clear that the University would continue to honor its contractual obligations to Brigham Young University but would re-examine its position when those obligations had ended. It was a well thought out response and did much to lay the issue to rest. Essentially the Black Student Union had made its case and while victory was not immediate it had, for all practical purposes won the battle. I am sure that, like most radicals who survived their causes, the majority of blacks involved have become stable members of society.

Chapter 9

University District Center:
Birth, Life, and Death

D uring the early seventies I became involved with the University District Center for transient and local youths.

The University District Center (UDC) opened on 20 January 1970. Had it been a child, the attending physician might have thought, "This kid doesn't look quite right. Neither do its parents."

The Center was a mish-mash of conflicting ideas concerning how to best serve the needs of the community. Should it take in AWOL soldiers, provide drug treatment, or cater more to straight young persons who were lost and uncertain in a tense world?

The persons behind the Center idea had been meeting since September 1969 and included ASUW president Steve Boyd, Walt Crowley, David Royer who headed the Campus Christian Ministry, Andy Shiga, a business man named Dick Leffel, John Mitsules, and me. Also included were other church youth workers and representatives from the Street People of whom Bill Harrington and Bob Shupe were the most active.

After meeting for several months we finally raised enough money through donations to commence the project.

Agreeing on articles and by-laws proved to be a time consuming process. In the fall of 1969 the University District Center was officially incorporated, a first step toward more adequate funding. The articles were signed by David B. Royer and William L. Harrington. The incorporators were Stephen L. Boyd, Walter C. Crowley and John Mitsules.

I arranged a nine month lease for a two story structure at 56th

The University District Center, 1970.

Street and University Way which was renewed in the summer of 1970. Dick Leffel was chosen as Interim Director.

There was little agreement as to objectives. To some the Center was a drugfree backfire against the flames of the drug revolution that appeared to be consuming young persons on the lower Ave. To others it offered an opportunity to shelter runaways and to provide methadone treatment and drug rehabilitation. The Center opened on 20 January 1970. The differing expectations of the community had been highlighted in the 19 December issue of the *Outlook*.

Dick Leffel anticipated that the street population would move to the Center when it wanted to but that it could not be pushed there. He spoke of job and housing referral, child care, psychological counseling, parent-child counseling, legal aid, and drug counseling. He foresaw that in the future the Center would house the Nation's first Methadone out-patient clinic for heroin addiction.

Bob Shupe, speaking for the street people, felt that the entire community should participate in the Center. Louise Wierman, a resident, was pleased that the Center would provide a place for young people to go, have coffee, see people, get help, and find out what was going on locally.

My statement, also printed in the *Outlook*, pretty much sums up my own view and that of the more liberal members of the business community.

> ...it would be very difficult to do anything for the hard core narcotic pusher who is simply an undesirable businessman operating outside the law. On the other hand, there are people who have dealt in drugs and narcotics who, to some degree, have done so under the force of economic circumstances. Consultation plus job referrals might be of assistance in reorienting these young people.
>
> Principally, however, I like to think of the Center as a place which will provide a focal point of interest primarily for young people who otherwise would be drifting, often without friends and usually without any significant purpose. It is to be hoped that the Center will provide them not only with communication and friendship among their own age group but also in finding jobs and medical and psychological referrals.
>
> ...It is very easy to look down your nose at these young people whose lives are bordering on the brink of disaster and blame all of their problems on them.

It is difficult for us to admit that somehow or other we have gotten our social structure so oriented that it has lost its appeal for some of our younger people. I do not think this is necessary and I believe that in establishing the Center we are demonstrating a real concern not only for the youth in our community but that there is a need for communication between all strata of our society.

Although Dick gave the Center his best shot the ambivalence of the Center's supporters and the lack of substantial financial support left Dick and the Center for the most part treading water.

Early in the summer of 1970, the Center temporarily closed for remodeling. Several of us including Dave Royer, John Mitsules, and Steve Boyd and me thought Walt Crowley should be the Director. John Mitsules had informally made arrangements for increased financial support from the City and a federal Law and Justice grant had been applied for. I had tapped a few private sources. We hoped that Walt could put the Center back on track.

We debated Walt's talents.

"Heck, he thinks no one should make more than 200 dollars a month."

"Offer him three and he'll become a capitalist."

We interviewed Walt who was already active in the Center. He was not only interested but his thinking ran parallel with ours. Namely, the Center would be an inviting place to stop in for coffee, read a book, or preach your particular gospel, watch a movie or attend a craft class. No drugs, no pushers, no runaways. We planned to serve the hundreds of young people, many of them wanderers, who were trying to find out what life was all about. We ultimately accomplished this with a network of homes as well as a hostel in the basement of the Baptist Church. Walt pointed out that if we catered to any other group, home hospitality would too often end in rip-offs and disaster.

On 28 September 1970 the *Daily* ran a story to the effect that there had been a turnover in the administration and personnel at the

Walt Crowley illustration on the cover of the UDC Annual Report, 1970.

Center. New paneling on the walls, tie-dyed curtains and spool tables were added. Soon a mural showing a great white breaking wave would engulf the north side of the building. Walt had, in fact, been calling the shots for several months including Wednesday night jam sessions with drop in musicians that started in August. It was during this period that Brare, the lad with the new teeth, supervised much of the construction and cut the half moon in the toilet door.

The policies of the Center changed abruptly. No more drugs or runaway children. With its library the main floor became a place to relax, have coffee, read, perhaps argue peaceably and carry on craft and other activities. On the second floor the Center office operated a network of home hospitality plus directing the operation of a major hostel in the basement of the Baptist Church. Job referrals were not unusual.

The Center lasted until 1972 but it was taken over by dissidents in November 1971.

My own relationship with the Center was an uplifting experience. I suspect some of them regarded me as a father figure and I felt the part. My memory of the Center is studded with happy recollections.

I negotiated the lease with a gentle Chinese man who had been a pharmacist. The Center had once housed a furrier who had constructed in the basement an almost impregnable vault. The pharmacist and I hit it off well and he confided that when he had closed his business he had stored the drugs, some of them highly desireable to drug users, in the vault. The lease required that only the Director have a key to the basement. I often chuckled to think what might have happened if some of our visitors had known what was under their feet.

The staff and Board Members met frequently in the Center's tiny office with most of us sitting on the floor. The first order of business was usually the adoption of a resolution baring Walt from smoking. Meetings often lasted until after midnight. We chatted about Center activities and about ourselves. Roxy Grant, for instance, kept us up to date on her pets which consisted of a boa constrictor that had the run of her house together with the white rats that met their fate in its coils.

There were giggles and then laughter on the night Roxy removed an upended sack and presented me with a foot high marijuana plant. After the meeting I reshrouded the plant and carried it down the stairs and out into the night while I debated its fate.

Driving down Brooklyn Avenue with the plant beside me I found the solution. Tom Coppage, a real estate broker who was both a friend and client maintained a small planting strip adjacent to his office building. Tom did not approve of my dalliance with radicals. Stopping in front of his building I planted the marijuana plant in the midst of his violets.

The night was not over. At home I proudly reported to Peg. "You did that to Tom?"

Digging up the plant at three a.m. while keeping an eye open for a patrol car could have ended in disaster. On the way home I dropped it off at the office.

For months it grew on the roof where it could not be seen. Then the Seattle *Times* covered a story about a single plant that netted its grower two years in jail. I gave the now two foot tall plant to Ruth, one of our secretaries, who kept it until her State Patrolman son-in-law ordered her to get rid of it. Ruth cut it up and returned it in an envelope. As far as I know it is still in the bottom drawer of my desk. Have I been tempted? Cookies or tea perhaps?

The Center's demise can be traced to an error made by many Community Councils and other activist groups. In the name of democracy, such organizations often have no dues or membership requirements and permit anyone coming to the annual meeting to cast a vote.

Had the Center been an individual it would be correct to say that it was buried in a pauper's grave. The November 1971 annual meeting was packed by a group calling itself the New American Movement. Claiming that the UDC structure was elitist and sexist the NAM dominated the meeting by electing eight of the ten new Board members and adopting a resolution that in the future the Board should be made up of half women and half men and at least two should be nonwhites. Only two blacks were present and their election was postponed to a subsequent meeting.

Walt tried to make the best of what was actually a fatal blow. The Center's grants were running out with little chance of renewal in the face of the takeover and its now obvious lack of direction. A mass meeting was held at the University Congregational Church. I did not attend but sent a secretary with a recorder. The tape proved to be an unintelligible Tower of Babel. After an evening of accusation, threats, and epithets it became evident that the Center was doomed. The fight was only over who should dispose of the carcass.

Before long two punks torched the Center's library. Lacking the support of its founders and without funds, the Center closed.

I resigned from the Center board on 13 June 1972. My comments in the letter of resignation in part illustrate the impasse which had been reached.

> I cannot help but feel that the Center at this point does present thorny problems which can only be resolved by our locking horns, a step I am reluctant to take both because I am not up to it and also I have become too fond of those involved in the Center to wish to start arguing with each other at this point.

> ...I feel that this Center has changed from a community oriented organization to one with a much more partisan approach. The fact that for two weeks it has had signs on the building such as 'Stay High,' 'Carve the Narks,' 'Street People Unite.' at a time when I have been trying to raise money for a hostel, has, in my judgement not only been unfortunate but almost amounts to sabotage of any hopes for a hostel this summer."... "Even though this paint job may have been done by someone with the mentality of a dodo bird and a rather low IQ, it seems to me that if the Center is to represent the entire community it should have been removed within 24 hours."

> ...One of the unwritten laws governing the Center is that we try and understand one another and that no one uses it to purvey his particular brand of philosophy.

I closed by expressing my willingness to work on Center problems relating to its original goals. In the end, the signs caused the cancellation of a 500 dollar grant for the hostel that I thought was in the bag.

Chapter 10

Kent State:
The Police Even the Score

Probably we should have prepared for trouble when on 4 May 1970, poorly trained Ohio National Guardsmen killed four students on the Kent State campus in Cleveland Ohio. Six days before, President Nixon had authorized the invasion of Cambodia.

In Seattle, two days after Kent State, several thousand marchers snarled Interstate 5. Amid much verbal abuse from the marchers, the police, who had been on 24-hour call, handled the situation professionally. The following day, 7 May, 10,000 demonstrators marched to the City Center without violence and with little vandalism. That night the University District was in agony.

Everyone anticipated trouble. Wearing white arm bands and with many carrying signs urging "non-violence," peacekeepers fanned out through the District. Many were graduate students, business persons, and street people. I was not there during the early hours, only at the finale. For the first time the target was the national administration, not the local business community.

On 7 May I was driving away from the District to an evening meeting. Something to do, as I recall, with my being chairman of the Seattle Planning Commission. I had turned on the police band but it was quiet. Then the call came from the dispatcher to the effect that all available units should move into the University District. "They are pouring gasoline into bottles in the parking lot on 15th N.E." This was half a block from the rear entrance to my office. This message

Kent State march in Seattle, on the freeway, 1970. Photo by Alan Lande.

proved to be an error on the part of the police, but I had no way of knowing that at the time. I was concerned that my own office could become a firebomb target.

I drove by the house and told Peg I was going to the office. She could hear the screaming sirens and felt very unhappy when I filled my pockets with shotgun shells.

I drove to the office uneventfully, and parked one street away on Brooklyn. The crowd was in the block to the south. As I jaywalked across the Ave to the office entrance, looking everywhere but where I was going I ran into the arms of George Gough, our beat officer. We both relaxed a bit and thought it hilarious. I was acutely aware of the shells bulging in my pockets and felt glad to escape up the stairs.

I could hear a disturbing crash and the tinkle of shattered window glass on the 15th Avenue side of the Pacific National Bank. Later I was to learn that this was carried out largely by one man, a motorcycle jock who hung around the University District Center. I never inquired and if I had it would have been fruitless, but reliable rumor has it that after bragging about his exploit he was thoroughly beaten by persons active in the University District Center. He ended up in the hands of the medics. (See letter to Reverend Walker in the Appendix)

I loaded Dad's 1891 double-barreled shotgun and sat in the dark for perhaps half an hour with the gun resting on the arms of the chair. I faced the darkened stairway waiting for the crash of glass below. Would I have had second thoughts if someone actually climbed the stairs? I never found out.

Soon I could hear only the rumble of the crowd. No boisterous yells, no sirens. I unloaded the shotgun and descended the dark stairway and joined the crowd in the 4300 block. They were older than on the previous riot. Many were University students, all were mature and their faces showed concern. There was an absence of the taunting attitude we had come to expect. They were also unaware of the nightmare many of them were about to experience.

I stopped at the northeast corner of the Ave and N.E. 43rd where a small group of students and a few faculty members were gathered. They were looking apprehensively back toward the Campus. "What's going on?" I inquired.

"The cops are on the campus. They've taken off their ID and

Kent State rally on the University of Washington campus, 1970. Photo courtesy Special Collections and Preservation Division, University of Washington Libraries.

they are beating up anyone they can catch. I even saw them pull some guy out of his car and work him over."

In the meantime Dick Coppage, President of the Chamber of Commerce, had joined the party.

Someone shouted, "Look out. Here they come."

Half a block away, members of the Tactical Squad were moving out of the alley and marching toward the Ave. A theater patron was about to enter his car. A squad member broke ranks, stepped into the street and bashed a dent in his car's fender with his club. Both Dick Coppage and I were reaching a slow boil. The others on the corner were leaving. We stayed.

The TAC squad crossed in our direction.

"Get going! You're obstructing the police."

"I'm——." A prod in the back sent me stumbling across the street toward what appeared to be a command post. Dick, similarly encouraged, was right behind.

A small crowd had been permitted to gather on the corner. It included my son-in-law who soon called Peg and told her not to worry if she should hear that I had been arrested.

Dick approached the officer in charge, who was not wearing his badge.

"What's your I.D. Number, Sergeant?" Dick inquired.

"Arrest him!"

After a brief discussion with my better judgement I decided to throw in my lot with Dick. Approaching the officer I got as far as "I'm the President of ....."

"Take this guy too."

Tim Stander from Mayor Uhlman's office intervened.

"You can't do that to these guys. One's President of the Chamber of Commerce and McCune's President of the University District Development Council."

"The hell we can't!"

Wrists strapped behind us in tight plastic handcuffs, we were shoved into a police car. The officers were dourly silent.

"Got any money?" whispered Dick.

"A couple of bucks maybe."

"Me too."

So much for making bail. In minutes the car stopped at the receiving office in the basement of the Public Safety Building. An officer approached the car.

"You got McCune and Coppage?"

"Yes."

"Take them back to the District and turn them loose."

The ride back without sitting on tight handcuffs was quite relaxing. We even tried, unsuccessfully, to kid the cops. Dick claims it was Assistant Chief Corr who overheard radio transmissions and ordered our release.

While we were being arrested Tim Stander took off on a run to the Meany Tower Hotel.

It was after ten o'clock. Police Chief Moore and the Mayor's buddy and mine, John Mitsules, had just ordered steaks and a drink. An agitated Stander broke in. "Chief, they've just arrested McCune and Coppage."

"I know McCune, he's a mean son-of-a-bitch. Who's Coppage?"

"President of the Chamber of Commerce."

"Oh, shit!"

According to Mitsules the Chief called headquarters. Part of the conversation included, "This is your Chief damn it. Now listen to me."

I have never understood what happened next. Mitsules and the Chief, apparently with the idea of giving Dick and me a bad time at the station, took off in the Chief's car. By the time they reached the Public Safety Building the criminals had already escaped. Thanks to Assistant Chief Corr we were already on our way back to the District. Tim Stander imbibed Mitsules's drink and ate the Chief's steak.

The night over, the process of sorting out the facts began.

One fact was clear. The "Vigilantes on Campus" proved to be primarily police. Members of HELP (Help Eliminate Lawless Protests) an organization that touted itself as being "the eyes and ears of the police," may have played a small part. If so, Chief Moore's investigation did not mention them. It had been primarily the police who had beaten up any person they could catch regardless of sex, arm bands or "No Violence" signs. The University Hospital treated twenty-five students and faculty members, many of whom required extensive embroidery. In one instance it worked in reverse. A plain clothes policeman, Leroy P. Reed, whom the University claimed was a vigilante, lost many of his teeth and suffered extensive facial injuries when he was clubbed in the mouth by a campus security officer. Reed sued the State of Washington and the security officer. His attorney argued that Robert Patton, the security officer, had used excessive force and had been inadequately trained. After a nine day trial the jury awarded Reed 25,000 dollars in damages.

Efforts to piece the facts together were hampered, perhaps almost of necessity, by O. E. Kanz, head of the campus police department. Not only did he refuse to be interviewed but apparently threatened with termination any campus officer who made a statement. Chief Moore appeared incredulous and adopted a "who us?" attitude. Frankly I think he was mad as hell and hoped the whole thing would go away. There was too much contrary evidence for Moore to sustain his position. Students were clubbed who had sought shelter in Terry Hall. A professor wearing a white arm band, Moncrieff H. Smith, was ordered by a Police Lieutenant to enter Terry Hall. Before he could do so he was shoved with a night stick and then hit over the head. Streaming blood he was pulled inside and an ambulance called. Professor Smith said he was appalled at the way both demonstrators and police behaved.

A female psychology student carrying a "No Violence," sign was clubbed and from the shelter of a telephone booth watched another girl being beaten. These instances and others have were described in the July 1970 issue of *Seattle Magazine*.

In the days that followed it became increasingly clear that "vigilantes" had arrived in city cars, and that they were carrying regulation night sticks, walkie talkies, and mace. There may have been a few outside vigilantes but this was never clearly established.

On 19 May a story in the Seattle *Times* credits Chief Moore with conceding that some of the vigilantes were plain clothes police officers. Moore, apparently for the first time, also expressed concern over a chain of command which permitted such officers to enter the campus in plain clothes.

On 4 June Chief Moore finally took action. Major Ray Carroll, a 21 year veteran on the force and head of special operations which included the tac squad was demoted to captain and transferred to another department. A Lieutenant and Sergeant were also transferred. Moore explained that to do more might have resulted in civil service claims which the city might lose.

Moore continued to point the finger at other unidentified groups of vigilantes saying it was under investigation. It was never denied that four tac teams each composed of eight men were on campus that night. Moore stated that the "over-reacting" consisted of officers "possibly" hitting people with night sticks and officers chasing demonstrators. According to the Seattle *Times*, Moore had previously taken the position that the only provable error was in permitting plain clothes tac squad members to carry night sticks.

The bright spot was that Moore appointed Dave Jessup, a very tough but honest and straightforward officer to succeed Major Carroll. Jessup made it quite clear that on his watch there would be no more funny business on the part of the tac squad. He stated that any man caught out of uniform or without his identification number would be recommended to the Chief for 30 days without pay.

I am convinced that Moore was sincerely distressed by what took place that night. I would have loved to overhear the dressing down I am sure he visited upon his chain of command.

On 8 May Mayor Uhlman closed the express lane on I-5 to permit protestors to return to the campus after 10,000 had marched by other routes to the Seattle Municipal Building. Except for sore heads, missing teeth, bad memories, a few broken windows, and irate motorists, the invasion of Cambodia and the Kent State killings were, if not forgotten, at least behind us.

In talking with today's students it is hard to convince them that it was anything other than a bad dream.

Chapter 11

The Mall:

An Idea Whose Time has Yet to Come

The lawyer's axiom "you win some, you lose some," applies with a vengeance to my participation in a three year project to save the major stores on University Way by developing a mall.

In 1969 Ernest Conrad on behalf of the University and Gordon Sweeney, the President of Safeco Insurance Company, asked if I would head up a group to try to solve the obvious deterioration of the Avenue. They proposed to raise 150,000 thousand dollars privately while the University would ante up an equal amount in the form of hiring a director and paying for office space and a secretary. Easily flattered, I agreed.

An illustration of the proposed mall.

Our touted supremacy as a "Department Store-Eight-Blocks-Long," was tarnishing. Our stylish women's specialty shops were closing. Stores such as Penny's, Kress, Woolworths and men's shops selling suites and ties were also closing, threatening to close, or moving to the more controlled situations to be found in commercial malls such as Northgate a few miles away and one of the first malls in the country. The University District was not alone. All along the west coast, malls were being undertaken as a panacea to revive dying businesses.

David D. Rowlands, a former City Manager of Tacoma, was hired as Executive Director. A non-profit corporation, the University District Development Council (UDDC), was formed, of which I was President. The Board consisted of members selected from the surrounding community and University faculty and staff. The University insisted that business representatives be in the minority.

At first our only identifiable opponent was the Community Council, an organization of residents with a Board elected at an annual meeting where anyone could vote. After election the board and officers pretty much pursued what they conceived to be the best interests of the community. The Community Council objected, not so much to the mall project but to those of us who were pursuing its goals. Bill McCord, President of the Council, argued that since public funds were involved, the administration should be left to a Board and officers elected at large by the community. Bill and I had a number of nasty confrontations. These usually took place at meetings of the Citizens Advisory Council (CAC) which we were instrumental in organizing in an effort to encourage citizen participation. At the CAC meetings I tried to point out that business representation was in a minority position on the UDDC board in spite of the fact that it was footing most of the bill and that the Board included more residents than business owners or operators. Bill would hear none of it.

Walt Crowley can be credited with what little encouragement the Community Council finally gave. He took over CAC as president early in 1972. On several occasions he told both Bill McCord and me to shut up. Walt engineered a community-wide door to door survey. We paid the out of pocket costs but nothing to Walt. I suspect he wrote it off as educational.

The completed survey showed overwhelming support for the mall. The Community Council was impressed but not sufficiently so to lend anything beyond grudging support. Had the Community Council been less obstructionist and had it attacked opposition to the mall rather than the effort to plan it, the end result might have been different and they would have been welcomed with open arms. It is difficult to second guess. Perhaps I was as stubborn as the other side.

By some illogical quirk of reasoning it never occurred to us that our principal opponents would come from among the business and property owners themselves. We knew there was opposition but badly misjudged its strength.

We first engaged the Richardson Associates, an architectural firm, now TRA, to supervise the preparation of an economic study. At a cost of 70,000 dollars we were told that such major stores as Penney's,

Kress, Woolworth, Diamond, Lerners, Helen Rickert, the Town Shop, Grinnel McLean, and Martin & Eckman would vanish unless bold steps were taken. The prophecy turned out to be accurate. Was it because the medicine in the form of a Mall was never taken? This is still a subject of debate.

Piloting the club plane, I visited every central city mall from Grand Junction, Colorado to Eugene, Oregon. In almost every instance before a mall had been considered stores were already abandoning the core of the city in favor of new malls in the suburbs. The idea of a center city mall was a rear guard action. The controlled environment of flashy suburban malls had too much to offer. I returned to most of the central city malls a year or two later. In spite of obvious enthusiasm in the beginning, for most of them their efforts were only ending in further dilapidation and decay.

Peg loyally documented the progress of our efforts in a scrapbook. I am amazed at the moving speeches I could make 25 years ago when my mind was somewhat more productive and I didn't need to worry about my false teeth falling out because I had forgotten to use the Poli-Grip.

More damaging to our own mall effort than the loss of the major retailers was the fact that landlords discovered they could cash in by renting a minimal space to a restaurant, a head shop, a hippie hangout, a pinball parlor or a franchise operation that cared little for the future of the Ave. While we worked to plan and sell the mall concept, rents, which were in jeopardy when we commenced our effort, doubled and trebled. We were in effect working to kill the cash cow landlords were milking.

Perhaps we were wrong and this change was the wave of the future. A few specialty shops such as import shops, brand name footwear, picture framing, a remarkable bead shop and a store selling Futons have found success on the Ave. Hopefully the balance will soon swing in that direction. There are some superb eateries with a foreign twist, a great college type tavern and excellent banking and other facilities. Other businesses, such as the drug stores are busy but dumpy, as compared with their glistening counter-parts in the malls.

Surveys show that today University students only occasionally visit the Ave except for businesses such as the banks, the University Book Store, Tower Records and a few specialty shops. The Ave has more than its quota of drug users, runaways, pan handlers, and drug pushers. After dark the Ave pretty much belongs to them.

Would it have been better or worse with a mall?. I now sit on the fence but properly policed and managed I think it might have worked. I make these comments primarily because today the surrounding residents are themselves looking at the possibility of a mall. Perhaps these observations will help.

By late 1972 it was too late to save the mall idea. The scale model on display in a bank lobby, the panels depicting various aspects of the mall, the support of all of the banks, the University Book Store, and Safeco were not enough.

The mall could only be established through a Local Improvement District. This would not prove feasible unless at least 51 percent, preferably 60 percent to cover property owners who might change their minds, signed up as favoring the mall. We sought out the property owners with our petitions. We knew that real estate broker and property owner, Don Kennedy, was violently opposed to the mall. We were not prepared for Don and several others taking to the Avenue and arguing that a mall would only create a haven for hippies and drugs. Were they right? After revisiting the California malls I concede that they may have been.

The signatures we secured in favor of the mall represented only 39 percent of the ownerships.

The mall idea was dead. On 16 December 1972 the papers carried a story in which I conceded defeat. My grief was tempered by a feeling that had haunted me the whole time. Almost a majority of our customers had come to the University District by automobile. Others had walked. Those coming by bus were in the minority. The proposed plan included no additional parking to offset several hundred parking spaces on the Avenue that the mall would have removed.

What could we have done to win? A more thorough selling job on my part would have helped. In addition, we lost Dave Rowlands at the end of the second year. As far as I could discover he had been verbally assured of a position at the University after three years with the UDDC. Dave had stirred up so much animosity on the part of the Community Council that the University told him they could not find a place for him. After he told me what had happened there was no choice but to tell him to take another job offer. Dave had a driving personality and an almost puritanical faith in his objectives. Had he been there to challenge the opposition it could have turned the tide.

FARMERS
MARKET

SATURDAYS

JUNE 3–
OCTOBER 28

9AM–1PM

50TH AND
UNIVERSITY WAY NE

BULLDOG
NEWS

NOBLE PALACE

MY'S
RESTAURANT

DESKTOP
PUBLISHING

PRINTING · CO

Chapter 12

How Now Brown Cow?

D issatisfied with "hunt and peck," I "borrowed" a typing manual
from the high school when I was fourteen and learned to type.
The "Quick brown fox" that "jumped over the lazy dogs" did not
impress me but "How now brown cow?" has stuck through the years.
Given a perplexing problem I say it to myself almost like a prayer.

I am doing so now. How does one end a book when the end is not
yet in sight? Today the community known as "The Ave," located one
block from the University of Washington campus, once the business
and social hub of the University District, virtually sits on a human
earthquake fault.

University Way, 1995. Photo by Priscilla Long.

In Seattle the streets in certain key business districts including the
Ave are rife with unrest, drugs, and disrespect for the law. They have
become home for those who have no place to seek shelter—to say
nothing of a youth counter-culture searching for friendship, excite-
ment and, all too often, drugs. It is no surprise that each week more
than 4000 clean needles are passed out by the needle exchange in the
few hours it operates on the Avenue.

Customers, fed up with beggars and with stepping around belligerent drunks and clusters of disaffected young people, have turned to
the malls for a more peaceful shopping experience. In Seattle's University District many buildings, some of them ancient converted houses,
are in disrepair. The business community finds itself befuddled by challenges that for many have proven disastrous. Others fatten on the sale
of 40 ounce bottles of beer or fortified wine and drug paraphernalia.
Shoplifting is endemic, usually by drug users.

As a landowner I feel qualified to comment upon the rent structure which in some respects shapes the type of business which can prosper on the Avenue. Store fronts which rented for 150 dollars per month in the 1960's now range from 1500 to 3000 dollars or more. Property values have risen in proportion. At first glance it would seem that higher rents would have winnowed out the less fit. Perhaps they did, but many of the less fit, low volume operations contributed to the Ave's delightful variety which failed to survive. They have been replaced by more than a score of ethnic restaurants, some of them excellent. Unfortunately most of their proprietors remain aloof from district concerns. Many of them are handicapped by English language difficulties that make complicated conversations difficult. Asians tend to mind their own affairs, rarely asking for help, even from the police. Somehow we must bring them into our family.

Many landlords have problems as great as their tenants'. For those of us who either inherited property or purchased it long ago, as did Peg and I for reasons earlier explained, it becomes only a walk to the bank. We can afford to be choosy about tenants and generous about rental and upkeep. But what about the investor who purchased 4,000 square feet for more than 600,000 dollars, rented it for 6,500 dollars per month and lost his or her tenant? As I write the space is still vacant.

What businesses form the spokes in the District's wheel? There are many. First must come the University Book Store followed closely by Safeco Insurance Company and the banks. These are both the most active participants and carry the largest financial burden. A host of other businesses make up the balance. Most of them are specialty shops or services. To name a few, Porter & Jensen, a jewelry store; La Tienda Folk Art Gallery, which the New York *Times* once commented was a "must visit" in Seattle; Monsoon, a bead shop whose owner annually searches the world; three excellent shoe stores; Shiga's, a truly oriental gift shop; Bulldog News, a panoply of world and local newspapers and magazines; two excellent photography studios; the best fish market in Seattle and Pitcher's, a massive floor covering store; a new Starbucks outlet; a collegiate micro-brewery; as well as other solid citizens like Radio Shack, camera and used book stores. Encouraging more of the same will help the Ave find a cure for its ills.

Those of us in business are prone to damn all of the so-called street people who inhabit the Ave. Perhaps this is our worst mistake. There are for instance the truly homeless. Many have psychological, drinking and drug problems. Others have been driven from their homes by abusive parents.

We often fail to realize that in addition to dealing with the seemingly permanent homeless we must consider a youth subculture that also exists on the Ave. The Ave is where the action is. Many among them insist on the right to lie and sit on our sidewalks, and to aggressively panhandle. They seem to delight in making old ladies uncomfortable.

Drugs still flow on the Avenue though perhaps less openly than in the 1960's. Head shops that peddle drug users equipment are slated for extinction by Prosecuting Attorney, Norm Maleng.

Many of the young people who hang out on the Ave might have stepped out of Star Wars, some with spiked and perhaps orange or purple hair, rings in their noses and often pierced eyebrows and tongues. This may not be an inspiring sight to many students and certainly not to a parent visiting the Ave. On the other hand, given our own youthful foibles, can we quarrel with this generation's desire to look funny?

An ancient philosopher viewing the scene from on high might well have difficulty accounting for the demands for free bread and board. He might well conclude, however, that for many this is just another generation acting hormonally stupid. If he interviewed me, for instance, I would have to admit that most of us wore our white corduroy pants until they were filthy black and our critics alleged they could stand unaided in a corner and emitted a very ripe odor. I lived in a basement room with only limited access to a laundry tub and toilet. On the other hand none of us expected a handout.

What are the crosses many business persons must bear as they look back over their shoulder and see short rations or insolvency not far behind?

"I can't keep them from shooting drugs in my restrooms" is a common complaint. "That damn drunk panhandler down the street that shouts "fuck you" at my customers," is another. "Who wants his kid attracted to that crowd of misfits blocking the sidewalks or to walk out in the street to go around them."

University Village, a mall, is located only blocks away. It provides stress free shopping with major stores, ample parking, and no beggars, sign carriers, or hand-bill posters. Five minutes north on I-5 the vast Northgate Mall does the same.

Even our sharpest retailer, the University Book Store, is panicked by a mammoth operation just opened by Barnes & Noble in University Village.

Yet such a sanitary mall might have limited attraction for the fiercely independent shopkeepers on the Avenue. All they really want is the right to do business unfettered by demands they cannot meet.

Both blocking the flow of pedestrians and restricting vehicular movement is a violation of the Loitering Ordinance. This has given the police a measure of control over situations in which people are blocking the entrance to a business, forcing customers to walk in the street or blocking traffic.

The future prospects of the street people who tarry on the Avenue are not good. They are under educated, possess no work history, carry chips on their shoulders, and suffer from home backgrounds that force some to move to the street, to say nothing of mental and drug problems. For many poverty lies ahead, as well as abusive spouses and "what might have been." It is no wonder that they cry for attention.

Fortunately there is often hope for the young. Three years ago a young teenage girl was required to perform community service in the Chamber office. Recently I found that she had been in foster homes and for several years was on the street. Two years later with a ring still in her nose, a steel stud in the tip of her tongue, and a baby to support, born while she was in a foster home, she now works part time and attends a Community College. Recently I observed a similar-appearing young woman doing an excellent job as a bank teller. Perhaps they represent a ray of hope for all of us.

Others in that age group are not underprivileged but simply change clothes and hairdos after school and hasten to the Ave. Lying and sitting on sidewalks they join the human clumps that make pedestrian passage difficult and uncomfortable. Many are simply passing through a phase in their lives.

More disturbing are the drunks and psychos who peer out from under a mat of tangled hair and demand attention. Panhandling ranges from a polite "Help feed my dog" to the unwashed bum who belligerently shoves a paper cup under the non-giver's nose and follows him or her down the street. The aggressive panhandling ordinance provides little protection. The prospective giver shuns a confrontation and in any event no officer is in sight. No wonder female employees often wish to be escorted after dark. Whether or not such fears are justified, the Ave has not been a place where anyone a bit squeamish would care to window shop.

How lucrative is panhandling? As far as we can determine it depends on the communication skills of the individual beggar. The person merely grunting and holding out a cup may be going hungry. But given the proper sales approach panhandling can be a money maker. Sources don't wish to be disclosed but when one panhandler left the street she was followed to a very expensive car. Her sign reading "Help feed my hungry children" puts money in the bank.

Much of the current activity of the business community as well as our hopes center on the Sidran Ordinance.

Sensing the City's plight Mark Sidran, Seattle's City Attorney, developed an ordinance which many of us feel is the best hope for making the Avenue liveable. The "Sidran Ordinance" was adopted by the City Council and approved by the Mayor after much soul searching and heated public debate.

The ordinance is rather simple.

Except for bus zones, and except for the disabled, and those who obtain a permit such as might be given to a restaurant for outdoor seating, it became illegal to sit or lie down on the sidewalk in business-zoned areas between the hours of 7:00 a.m. and 9:00 p.m. including the use of a chair. The ordinance made a number of exceptions such as parades conducted under permit. It requires that the police give a warning before a person is cited. It does *not*, as often claimed by its opponents, forbid panhandling.

Mainstream churches dot the district. Many of them are intent on providing food, shelter, and counseling. The Chamber of Commerce and various service clubs have contributed generously to their efforts. Probably these business-oriented supporters, as well as the churches, saw only the good which might result from their efforts. Yet the churches, or their operating groups such as the Greater Seattle Council of Churches together with the Displacement Coalition, and the ACLU, along with organizations having a Communist or Socialist bent, belligerently condemned the Sidran ordinance. Marches, sidewalk sit-ins and minor near-riots were their bill of fare. Free food and shelter for street people appear to be the price to be paid for a pleasant pedestrian experience.

Many young people on the street are complying with the Sidran ordinance and perhaps realize that by observing modest restrictions on their activities their lives can be made both more orderly and stress free. The proprietor of an electronics store comments that he feels more comfortable with the young people who no longer bunch up on the sidewalk outside his store and that they too appear more aware of his need to make his customers feel at ease.

In the sixties and seventies a manifesto from the street might conclude, "Anarchism Forever!" Today the handbills may be just as vicious but they rest on other grounds, the Constitution.

Today it is argued that a man sprawled on the sidewalk, is engaging in a constitutionally protected act of free speech with his tangled hair and unkept appearance, even though he is beyond verbal communication.

Until the recent legislative session the problem was complicated by 1970's legislation foreclosing the right of the police to pick up minors if they are runaways and hold them for their parents or in the Juvenile Center. Recent legislation has restored what had formerly been considered rights on the part of both the police and parents. A ten year old can no longer thumb his or her nose at the police with impunity.

Many on the Ave complain loudly of police harassment. A close examination, however, would support the conclusion that this is untrue. There was a day when a police John Bircher had no qualms about accompanied visits to the alley or whacking his victim where it hurt. As I have recounted, I myself once took an unsolicited ride in a prowler car. Today the police on the Avenue are enforcing the Sidran Ordinance. But they are doing so cautiously and fairly. The only way to discourage them is to scream "harassment." This problem has been eased. For the first time the city has community service officers who oversee community relations.

Other precincts may not be so fortunate. Gilbert and Sullivan concluded that, "A policeman's lot is not a happy one." We are lucky in the North Precinct. In at least some other precincts trying to talk to a policeman is difficult. The result is often a grunt and a gimlet eyed appraisal that brings on guilt feelings. Perhaps he too is frightened. Possibly he had a civilian friend who woke him at midnight. "My brother just got picked up for beating up a neighbor. Could you find out how much trouble he's in?" In such precincts both sides might benefit from a coffee drinking seminar, though probably not from "smoking a joint together" as was once suggested by a street leader.

There is no magic remedy. While much rests upon the fate of the Sidran Ordinance, even more depends upon our own ability to make the district attractive. How do we go about it? First we in some way establish a feeling of responsibility on the part of what society erroneously lumps together as "the homeless" and particularly we must come to terms with their supporters. Both the City administration and the community must recognize that the price paid by businesses throughout the City is too high and that we are being asked to work in a jungle dominated by a few persons dedicated to being destructive non-participants. No one will benefit from an Ave of vacant store fronts and boarded up businesses. Fortunately free enterprise dictates that the doors soon open and the windows are polished as a successor with a new formula tries for success.

Perhaps I am too dispirited. A spark of hope is flickering that could flame into at least a partial solution. It is based in large part upon the following hypothesis: make the Avenue attractive with improved lighting, and new and slightly wider sidewalks; encourage new businesses with wide public appeal; curtail the activities of delis selling 40 ounce bottles of beer or fortified wine; establish a location for police to prepare reports and meet the public; control graffiti; and above all, encourage businesses and landlords to improve their building facades. Then select tenants suitable for a broader mix of human needs and interests.

We are on the move. Master minded by a volunteer, Patty Whisler, formerly head of the city's Neighborhood Services Division, goals are falling into place. She has enlisted participation by Community Councils, the Chamber, the City Planning Department, business and property owners and residents.

Several professors in the University of Washington Department of Urban Planning and Design and the Department of Architecture have assigned their classes the task of redesigning the Avenue. Over several quarters they have come up with a grabbag full of thought provoking and often very practical ideas. Can the Ave be reworked in such a way that all of us, including the homeless, will take pride? Drop by and look for signs of progress.

Most of my compatriots have drifted away. Those older than I are deceased. The rest of us reminisce when we meet and resurrect our dimming memories. I am the only old timer still carrying the flag in the University District. John Mitsules has retired from his position at the Woodland Park Zoo. Andy Shiga died in 1993. Dave Royer is a minister. President Odegaard is writing his own reminiscences. Vice President Ernest Conrad died in 1994. Walt Crowley is also writing a book about the 60's and we often compare notes. Paul Dorpat's camera continues to click and he has a weekly historical story in the Seattle Times. The activists in the Center have gone in all directions. Roxy married a stockbroker. Brare recently visited my office and left his phone number, which didn't work when I tried it. Some day, if he reads this, I hope he will visit again. Dick Leffel purchased a University Way apartment building with storefronts and carried out a gaudy but intriguing restoration.

My high school buddy, Buster Meakins, died in 1992. He rode a tractor until he had a stroke. He was the last link to my youth in Haxtun. Bus and I had once dreamed of ourselves as jointly raising wheat in northeastern Colorado. Our meetings in later years were mostly concerned with, "what might have been."

My father died in 1964. You may want to skip this part. I suppose that in some sense I am crying on the reader's shoulder. Dad died on the second floor of the Drake Mercantile Building which, after Dr. McKnight had moved our old house to Sterling, had been converted from an apartment house to a hospital. It was early October. The window was open and in the street below the annual Corn Festival was in full swing. From the window I could see the firehouse where for years Dad had presided over the corn exhibits.

I was alone with Dad. From time to time a nurse would look in, I assume to see if he had passed away. I tried to talk but words were difficult. Finally he grasped my hand as firmly as he could and was gone. The doctor told me that with an injection he could keep my father alive for, at most, two days.

Now I regret saying "No." It would have given me an opportunity to tell him something I had always wanted to say but never did, "Dad, I love you very much."

Funeral arrangements posed a problem. Dad wanted to be cremated. When Wes and I told Wes's old classmate, Junior Radford, the town undertaker, that we wanted cremation his response was, "For God's sake don't do that to me. No-one in Haxtun has ever been cremated. We spared Junior and the last thing I did on the night before the funeral was to roust him out and have him open the casket while I inserted my parents love letters.

The day of the funeral wasn't easier. Ellen, Dad's widow, had turned down a Masonic delegation eager to put on a show, telling them vehemently that Dad had been a member for more than fifty years and not a single Mason had visited him during his final siege in the hospital. Wes and I were proud of her.

I remember little of the trip to the Cemetery. When we returned to the Methodist Church the Ladies Aid served lunch. The reminiscences were laudatory but I can remember only one. The State Patrol had a long bout with Dad and had gradually curtailed his driving. The graveled roads left Dad with an aggravating habit of driving on whichever side was the easiest travelled. At the time of his death it was limited to 20 miles from Haxtun. I overheard a man at my table comment to another, "Thank God, McCune's off the road at last."

It is perhaps time to say goodbye to this account of the life I have savored as well as to the reader, at least those among you who have had the stamina to follow me down what must have been a tortuous trail. There is little that I would change. Perhaps I'll stick around for a few more years as an overpopulated world bubbles and boils. Today I walked the Avenue. It was the opening day of a new term. My mood was lifted by the eager faces, the spontaneity, and different races walking together. I wondered if 100 years from now we all might be a little darker or lighter.

CHAOS!

ICE CREAM CAN MAKE YOU STERILE!

Our local homo copus (copsuckess) have declared war upon "hippies". (Defined as those with long hair). THE CHURN IS WORKING HAND-IN-CROTCH WITH THE POWERS-THAT-BE!

DESTROY TO BUILD! Block Traffic!

The dialog is over--
When the music's over
TURN OUT THE LIGHTS!
this leaflet P. T. A. the organization. produced by P. T. A. of schizoid surrealism

THE URGE TO DESTROY IS A CREATIVE URGE!

SABATOGE

ANARCHY!

Here is a reproduction of a flier handed out on the Ave in the late sixties.

Appendix

This appendix contains documents intended not to be comprehensive but to reflect the flavor of the sixties and early seventies in the University District. Dozens of bitter interchanges as well as attempts at persuasion have not been included. Several letters deal with the rise and fall of the University District Center. Of major importance were my activities during and after the Kent State riots as reflected in a letter to the Center.

This is the statement made by the University District Chamber of Commerce in response to the riot in August 1969.

Statement of the University District Chamber of Commerce

Approved by Board Action
and Released by C. M. McCune, its Legal Council
on August 14, 1969

Perhaps it is because our business district is close to a University that we have been more tolerant than would perhaps normally be the case in dealing with those among our young people who are having a difficult time adjusting within a society from which they feel alienated. The result has been that some people have taken advantage of this situation to engage in illegal activities on University Way, consisting largely of the sale of drugs and narcotics. We have tried since its inception to discourage this illegal activity with only limited success.

The police tend to blame leniency on the part of the courts and the courts in turn appear inclined to feel that the police have not taken advantage of all of the enforcement tools available to them.

In any event, the merchants whose businesses are most seriously affected are frankly, not too much impressed with the argument on the part of the young people that they legally are entitled to loiter on the sidewalk and use the streets for the illegal sale of drugs, whether the merchant is forced out of business or not. Even the fact that every morning merchants must sweep up the litter left on the street the night before cannot help but be irritating. Broken windows and other forms of harassment have been the fate of several merchants who have complained of conditions on the Avenue.

On Wednesday morning it was called to our attention that a mass meeting was to be held on the University Campus, the notice of which we secured a copy. Deleting the four letter words, a portion of its language was as follows:

> "It's been the same thing at Alki in West Seattle. Last Sunday the people said _____! Stoned some pigs and pig cars and burned one pig car out."

> "A small number of people in this country have a whole lot of power and they're using their pigs and their army to keep that power."

> "The people at Alki, Park Lake, Lake Hicks, Golden Gardens, the Ave. and all over the city have got to come together just like they did last Sunday and Monday."

> "Wednesday night the brothers and sisters are getting together again at 7:30 up on Hippie Hill (NE 42nd and 15th NE). Let's be there. The time has come to bring the war home! Get it on!"

In the face of this provocative type of hand bill we were of course very much concerned that damage might occur to businesses and injuries occur to young people in the district.

We are not critical of the way in which the police department handled the situation. They were criticized at Alki because it was argued they provoked the acts of vandalism. The error of such an accusation was clearly proven last night. There was not a uniformed policeman in sight until at least 15 minutes after the burglar alarm went off at the Bluebeard as it was being looted. It is, of course, difficult for businessmen to actually watch such a looting and wonder why police protection is not more adequate. Perhaps we had to suffer simply to demonstrate the fact that these people are out to provoke the police and will commit whatever crime is necessary to bring them to the scene if they are not already there. How such situations should be handled in the future is a police matter. They have our full support.

It does seem to us, however, that where there is an assembly which clearly has for its purpose the incitement of a breach of the peace, the organizers and promoters of such an activity should be subject to arrest. Certainly their identities must be known.

Second, we question whether or not after a meeting on the campus where such incitement to riot takes place, the people involved should be allowed to return to University Way, and then to stand around until someone throws the first rock or breaks in the first door.

If it is hoped that by this harassing action the district will change its attitude toward the pushing of drugs and narcotics, we want to make it clear that such a change will not occur. We also want to make it clear that we will continue to be a community that tries to understand the problems of today's youth.

As far as vandalism, window breaking and looting are concerned, we feel that the police department should use all and any force which is reasonably required to prevent such an occurrence again.

The very fact that a store could be looted, the contents carried half a block and secreted in a car and the looters mingle again with the crowd makes it obvious that the police leaned over backwards to avoid a provocation. We do commend the police department for the restraint used once they were on the scene and controlling the situation.

Here are the contents of four incendiary handbills passed out in the University District in the late sixties. The original spelling has been retained. The format reproduces as closely as possible the format of the original flier.

Meeting of the Street People

thur - Aug. 21 4 p.m.

hippy hill

1.the demand has been made that hardwick, finkner and theor commanding seargent be removed from the street,

a. that the number of beat police working between 39th and 45th be limited to two (2) and no more.

b. that plain clothesmen be eliminated on university way.

2.the formation of a committee composed of street people, students, merchants, and the beat police that are assigned to university way; for the purpose of handling the problem of police harassment and working together toward the ideal of disarming beat police (to a short stick and a radio between 39th and 45th) has been demanded.

3.the situation in the u. district has been allowed to cool off but many of us face jail sentences in connection with the police instigated riots of wednesday and thursday nights. for these people amnesty is being demanded.

these demands have been presented to the merchants and the police and the city government and have been recognized by them as ideas to be discussed and considered.

the real question here is that of the problem of police harassment and how it should be combated.

how can these demands be furthered

can we of the street get behind these demands?

thus far in a series of six meetings with the establishment (cops merchants and government) there has been no tangible action taken in the direction of potentiating these demands.

if at the next such meeting (which will take place thursday night 8 pm at the hub - tomorrow) there is no positive indication that these demands are being taken seriously, what action should we of the street persue?

WE ARE PEACEFUL PEOPLE, BUT IF WE ARE ATTACKED WE WILL RETALIATE.

THE PIGS LEARNED THAT THIS WEEK.

WHEN WE FIGHT, WE FIGHT TO WIN, NOT TO GET WIPED OUT. LAST NIGHT THE PIGS, THE PLAINCLOTHES PIGS, AND THEIR MOTHERFUCKER VIGILANTES WERE READY FOR US. BUT WE WERE NOT READY TO FIGHT THEM. TO DEFEAT THE PIGS, WE HAVE TO BE ORGANIZED, WE HAVE TO CATCH THE PIGS BY SURPRISE, AND WE HAVE TO HAVE WEAPONS EQUAL TO THEIRS. WHEN WE FIGHT, WE FIGHT TO WIN, NOT TO GET WIPED OUT.

OUR OBJECTIVE IS NOT TO LOOT THE MERCHANTS. WE DON'T WANT MOST OF THEIR SHIT ANYWAY. WHEN WE WANT SOMETHING FROM THE PIGS WE WILL GET ORGANIZED AND MAKE THEM SERVE OUR NEEDS. WE DON'T WANT THEIR COLOR T.V.'S.

WE WANT LAND, BREAD, HOUSING, DECENT EDUCATION, CLOTHING, FREEDOM AND PEACE. WE HAVE TO ORGANIZE THE POWER OF THE PEOPLE TO DEFEAT THE MAN. WE HAVE TO HOLD MEETINGS—MASS MEETINGS IN OUR COMMUNI-TIES—TO TALK TO THE PEOPLE ABOUT OUR NEEDS. WE HAVE TO WRITE PAPERS, SHOW FILMS AND TALK WITH THE PEOPLE.

IF WE HAVE MOVED THE PIGS OFF OUR STREET, THEN THIS IS THE TIME TO GET ORGANIZED. PEOPLE FROM OTHER COM-MUNITIES SHOULD NOT COME OUT HERE TO BRING THE PIGS DOWN ON THIS COMMUNITY—THEY SHOULD ORGANIZE THEIR OWN COMMUNITIES.

"FIGHT NO BATTLE UNPREPARED, FIGHT NO BATTLE YOU ARE NOT SURE OF WINNING; MAKE EVERY EFFORT TO BE WELL PREPARED FOR EACH BATTLE, MAKE EVERY EFFORT TO EN-SURE VICTORY IN THE GIVEN SET OF CONDITIONS..."

THE PIGS HAVE SHOWN US THAT "POLITICAL POWER GROWS OUT OF THE BARREL OF A GUN"

—MAO TSE TUNG

CHAOS !

ICE CREAM CAN MAKE YOU STERILE!

Our local homo copus (copsuckers) have declared war upon "hippies".
(Defined as those with long hair). THE CHURN IS WORKING HAND-
IN-CROTCH WITH THE POWERS - THAT - BE!

DESTROY TO BUILD!

BLOCK TRAFFIC!

The dialog is ours -

(When the music's over)
(TURN OUT THE LIGHTS !)

This leaflet produced by P.T.A. the organization of schitzoid surrealism
A N A R C H Y !

WE WALKED OUT

Representatives of the police department have committed themselves to end the harrasment in the streets, the harrasment continues!

Representatives of the merchants have said that they want an end of police harrasment in the district. the harrasment continues!

LIARS AND LIES! LIARS AND LIES! LIARS AND LIES!

The police force and the police violence which was directly responsible for the riots of three weeks ago continues unrelented. The use of fraudulent and false charges, warrant and I.D. checks, police arrogance and police harrasment continues unabated.

In meetings that we have had with the representatives of the city government, with representatives of the police force, and with representatives of the merchant community of the district we have been given sweet words and honeyed promises - - but the violence of the police continues.

It is obvious that many of these people regard the meetings themselves as a way of cooling things off and do not intend any actual reforms to emerge from these meetings. We refuse any longer to be a party to this charade. As long as our brothers and sisters continue to be busted and harrassed by the police talk becomes nonsense.

AS LONG AS
MASSIVE HARRASMENT CONTINUES ON THE STREET
THE PEOPLE OF THE STREET MUST DEFEND THEMSELVES
IN THE STREET!

The Street Caucus

Here is the letter I wrote to the Director of the University District Center after my arrest in the spring of 1970.

May 9, 1970
University District Center
5525 University Way N.E.
Seattle, Washington 98105

Attention: Dick Leffel, Director

Dear Dick:

After I managed to get myself busted on Thursday night along with the esteemed President of the University District Chamber of Commerce, it seems wise to reiterate some of my philosophy to the members of the Center. I fear that if I do not, the feeling of unjustified approbation which I detect may lead to future disappointments.

In the first place I shall continue to do my best to be a mean son of a bitch who unfortunately likes people. The fact that these range from policeman and business types to ex-pushers and a few S.L.F.'rs makes life complicated.

Secondly, I am very much a law and order type of guy. To me the accomplishments of a lifetime, whether in the form of a business, a house, a personal library, or his community are as much a projection of a man as an arm or a leg. I feel he should be willing to kill or be killed in their defense. On Thursday I was simply applying this philosophy to the University District where I started as a dishwasher almost forty years ago.

I can imagine Walt Crowley pointing out that a man's convictions are a much more important projection of himself than these mere physical trappings. If so, he would be right. To the extent that a man might be defending his personal right to assert his views and not to cow others into following the same path, I would be in agreement.

Thursday night I came back to my office after tuning in the police band and hearing a report that "molotov cocktails" were being made on 15th N.E. a half block away. Quite frankly, I would have either arrested or shot the first guy to break in the door.

Later I went out on the Avenue and started to thank some of the people with arm bands for tying to "cool it." In the course of doing this, I ran into Dick Coppage and we wandered down to 43rd and University Way where the tactical squad was marching around. I got in a discussion with some students about vigilantes and tried to assure them that it wasn't anything more than an S.L.F. stratagem to stir up more trouble. Unfortunately, I began to get a sick feeling they were right and also what group might be involved.

My usual nasty disposition was not improved when at this point a tac squad member across the street clobbered the fender of a car with his club for no reason at all that I could see except to intimidate the driver. In a couple of minutes the squad came by the corner and told us to get off the street. I got shoved fairly hard and when we got across the street, Coppage said that as President of the Chamber of Commerce he felt he had a right to stay on the street. He asked to talk to a sergeant. That did him in.

I was about twenty feet away and had to decide whether to try and rescue Dick, realizing that if I failed, we would both be on the way to the pokey. I told them who we both were, was told to get going and finally asked the officer for his serial number. I don't recommend nylon cord handcuffs for every day wear.

I am not complaining. If the police have the right to clear the streets, as distinguished from disbursing a crowd, without a Mayor's declaration of emergency, we both had it coming. In any event every one was up tight.

I think if we are going to join hands to try and work with and to understand and sympathize with students, drug users, radicals and business men, we owe the same duty to the police. At least I will make a sincere effort as soon as I cool off a bit more over their hitting that guy's car.

My own delightful evening is water over the dam. There are, however, a couple of points I wish to raise.

A number of professors, students and Center Members were on the Avenue trying to cool the situation. Without them, I am sure the damage would have been ten-fold greater. While the police may be right that the white arm band wearers were infiltrated by rock throwers, I saw no indication of this. Some protestors were wearing the bands to indicate a peaceful intent.

The police or vigilantes clobbered some of these people pretty badly. At the next meeting of the "harassment Committee" I hope someone will raise holy hell about this and set up some system to assure police cooperation with students and citizens. We didn't have any of it Thursday. Unfortunately, the police feel they have no public support and that they are not backed up by the courts. This feeling of insecurity led to some of the things that occurred on Thursday night. It seems to me that we must recognize that only the police can stand between us and either anarchy from the left, or vigilantes from the right. We can help with arm bands and student resistance to violence, but these alone are not enough. Somehow we must bring the entire community to the conclusion that violence not only is inappropriate, but must be dealt with in a legal way. The only alternative is more cracked heads and broken windows.

As far as the vigilantes are concerned, I don't think the Center should belabor the issue at this point. The word I get is that the wheels are already turning. I think we should also have a talk with the S.L.F. Can you get me an invitation to dinner at one of their collectives?

Sincerely,

Cal McCune

P.S. If anyone gets the idea I'm a radical, you can tell him what a bastard I am and let him read this letter.

This letter to a church pastor defends members of the University District Center who seriously beat a bragging biker who had broken all the windows on the east side of the University Bank.

June 8, 1970

University United Methodist Temple
1415 N.E. 43rd
Seattle, Washington
Attn: Dr. Daniel D. Walker

Dear Dan:

Thanks for your though provoking letter of June 3rd.

I am personally rather inclined to agree with you that it is unfortunate that the culprit referred to in your letter could not be handled through the proper authorities. There are several reasons why in this case such action was impossible.

The individual involved was a loud mouthed out-of-towner, probably strung out on drugs, who apparently bragged about what he had done when he visited the Center. Aside from the fact that, as I get it, the young people who had conversations with him felt that he was probably telling the truth, there would be no way in the world to take any legal action based upon his obvious braggadocio. I do feel sure, however, that if such a person were to come to the Center and brag about something he was going to do of this nature, more formal action would be taken by the members of his peer group with whom he would be talking.

The other factor which militates against more authoritative action is that the Center functions by volunteer basis due to lack of funds and at this point it would be pretty difficult to lay down firm enough ground rules to force disclosure, assuming this to be advisable.

In short, what happened was that, as far as I can find out, some of the leaders at the Center learned that the young man involved had been making statements about window breaking activities. This was somewhat after the fact, and I am not sure that his identity was disclosed to anyone having any authority. I am sure that if I tried to obtain it, it would be refused, but I am equally sure that the gentleman involved was told by his own peer group that such type of activity was not welcomed, nor was he welcome at the Center.

How to handle situations of this kind is a very difficult question when one is trying to reach a group which could very easily go out and do the same thing with a little encouragement from the radical Left. What we are trying to do is to eliminate this kind of activity, and I am really convinced that this was handled in the best way that it could be under the circumstances. I would suggest that you might want to discuss this type of situation with Dave Royer, who is now president of the U. District Center and who, I am sure, is concerned about the approach it takes to this type of problem.

Sincerely,

C.M. McCune

———————————

In November 1971 I wrote to Walt Crowley after the annual meeting of the University District Center was packed by members of the dissident group, New American Movement. It was another few months before I resigned.

November 12, 1971
Mr. Walter Crowley
University District Center
5525 University Way N.E.
Seattle, Washington 98105

Dear Walt:

I hand you this letter with sorrow in my heart and the hope that you will not have occasion to use it.

Events of last Monday evening will, I am afraid, forever dim what has been an increasingly bright light of mutual understanding and community of interest in the University area.

I see no way that this can be avoided unless those who are attempting the takeover of the Center can be persuaded to play a role as a partner in the operation of the Center within the framework of its stated purposes.

We have all along felt that we were losing touch with the radical sector of the community, and did make efforts to incorporate them into the Center without, at the same time, making it the foundation for espousing ideological causes or political activity. Indeed, had we done these things, it could not have survived as long as it has, and would not have qualified for non-profit status under the IRS.

If this coalition of outside groups insists upon the fulfillment of its expressed intention of taking over control of the Center with the obvious purpose of radicalizing it to a point where any support received from the community would be given under duress, then I am afraid we must part.

If on the other hand they can align themselves with the purposes of the Center, recognizing that it was formed on the concept that no one group would have control, as is suggested by the Bylaws, then I would be more than happy to continue on the board, even though I may be, as I frequently am now, outvoted on many issues.

Another factor which I cannot overlook is that though I must confess that I enjoy argumentative confrontation, taken to excess it has been and would be detrimental to my health, and I am afraid I am coming close to my tolerance level.

It has been no sacrifice for me to devote as much time as I have to the Center, and indeed I feel that I am much in its debt, even though some of my more conservative clients may think my activities bordered on lunacy. Certainly it has changed my views and opened up many aspects of life in terms of human relationships. At my age, it is not surprising that I should now develop a fatherly feeling for young people with whom I have been so closely associated. Indeed, I must confess that I have developed a strong bond of affection for persons whom I would have spurned only a few years ago. I only regret that more members of the business community could not have shared in this experience.

I did not intend that this should be a tear-jerker, but I am afraid that is the way I feel, realizing that the time may come when we must again take separate paths.

Finally, I would like to express on behalf of those of us in the business community who have been interested in the Center our appreciation for what the Center staff has done to promote understanding in the community.

I would be the first to recognize that we have not supported the Center in the financial way as we should have done. Knowing the business community, however, and the suffering that it went through, emotionally and financially, at the hands of those who have held attitudes very similar to, and in some cases identical with, those persons who were at the meeting on Monday night, I perhaps have more sympathy for their position than would some.

At the same time, I must recognize that those of us in the business community were all too willing to overlook the problems with which young people were trying to deal, and to condemn them, for their concerns. Perhaps had it not been for the drug scene, which we all agree was horribly bad, their attitudes might have been somewhat different. Even there, our lack of understanding of the problems involved and the depth of those problems made it difficult for us to work together with the street people and the students.

Many of these attitudes and misconceptions on both sides have been overcome by the Center, and I think perhaps that both the University District business community and our young people have a better understanding of each other than would be found in almost any other university community.

I hope that we will not lose this understanding, and that it somehow can be increased. I also hope, and I fear it is only that, that you will not find it necessary to tender this resignation on my behalf.

Yours truly,

C.M. McCune

———

I resign from the Center when radicals take over and erect plywood signs painted with slogans such as "Stay High" and "Carve the Narcs."

June 13, 1972
University District Center
5525 University Way N.E.
Seattle, Washington 98105
Attention: Roxie Grant, Director

Dear Roxie:

I am afraid the time has come when I must with considerable regret resign as a member of the Board of Directors of UDC. There are several reasons for taking this step which I hope the Board and the staff will understand.

In the first place, I am involved as you know, as president of the University District Development Council in trying to work out a mall installation on University Way. This has entailed a good deal of confrontation that has frankly run my blood pressure up to a point where I must curtail some of my activities.

I cannot help but feel that the Center at this point does present some thorny problems that can only be resolved by our locking horns, a step which I am reluctant to take both because I am not up to it and also because I have frankly grown too fond of those involved in the Center to wish to start arguing with each other at this point. I therefore feel it would be better to make way for someone else on the Board and to continue to support the Center in those activities I feel are important to the community.

I do feel, however, that I should set forth some of the views which I hold and which affect my attitude toward the Center as it is now operating. In summary, these are as follows:

1. I feel that this Center has changed from a community oriented organization to one with a much more partisan approach. The fact that for two weeks it has had signs on the building such as "Stay High", "Carve the Narcs", "Street People Unite", at a time when I have been trying to raise money for a hostel, has in my judgment not only been unfortunate but almost amounts to sabotage of any hopes for a hostel this summer. On the other hand I don't want to appear to be dictating what the staff should do. I simply want to point out that people support the things which they consider worthwhile and which they believe contribute to the community. Anyone driving by the Center at this time would have grave doubts as to the purpose for which it was operated and if they had been involved in it as an effort to achieve a common meeting ground of all facets of the community, they would probably break down and cry. Even though this paint job may have been done by someone with the mentality of a dodo bird and a rather low IQ, it seems to me that if the Center is to represent the entire community it should have been removed within 24 hours.

The fact that such businesses as the University Publishing Co. don't remove this type of signing does not reflect on the organization as it does on the Center where we are already suspect in many quarters.

2. One of the unwritten laws governing the Center is that we try to understand one another and that no one uses it to purvey his particular brand of philosophy. I feel that this concept no longer applies to the Center and frankly unless it can be a voice for community consensus, agreement and understanding, I would prefer not to remain on the Board even though I will show a continuing interest in the Center and support it in those activities which continue to carry out its original purposes.

3. I suppose I am particularly irked because for the past month I have been nursing along a possible $500.00 donation toward the hostel program. Many members of the Board of the organization I have been working with travel along University Way almost daily and unfortunately they have seen the signs

now on the lower portion of the front of the Center and my efforts are very likely to come to naught. I am hoping that these signs can be removed before their board meeting tomorrow night. I have already told them I was sure this was not the work of the Center's staff, which I hope was correct, but the fact that the staff apparently condones it makes it difficult.

This has been a difficult letter to write. Many of us have spent a vast amount of time and energy trying to develop the Center as a crossroads for the community. Perhaps the most valuable thing it has done for me is to broaden my own perspective and to afford me an opportunity to enjoy an acquaintanceship with today's young people and in some measure to understand their problems and concerns. That we have not been able to enlist more support in the community at large in both an understanding and financial nature has been a source of disappointment to myself and many others. That understanding and the participation of a broader spectrum of the community are goals which I think the Center should continue to pursue.

One further point, the Center is charged with certain duties under its lease, one of which is to restore the premises in as good a condition as they were received. While we have made many improvements to the premises, I would hope that in the few remaining months of the lease the property will be adequately maintained. I would also hope that there will be no violations of the lease, such as using the premises for crashing, no matter how desirable this might be.

Let me also say that if the Center does have problems with which I can assist I hope that they will continue to call upon me, irrespective of whether or not we agree that the original goals of the Center are being supported, or the fact that we may have differing political views.

Yours truly,

C.M. McCune

Index

A

American Civil Liberties Union (ACLU), 135.
Anderson, Loren "Andy," 20.
Armstrong, Louis, 29.
ASUW (Associated Students of the University of Washington), 63.

B

Bannister, Del, 15.
Barnes & Noble, 134.
Becker, Mae, 16.
Bell, Charles (great grandfather), 7-8, 49.
Bell, James (grandmother's brother), 7, 9.
Bell, Margaret (great grandmother), 8.
Beloin, Lillian, 77.
Bentson, Ellen, 21, 139.
Beyer, Richard, 86.
Bissel, Trim and Judith, 101-102.
Black, Justice Hugo, 49.
Black Panthers, 76, 92.
Black Student Union, 65, 106-107.
Blankenship, Miles, 74.
Blue Beard (store), 95.
Blue Moon Tavern, 60, 61, 68, 80.
Bon Marche (store), 34.
Bookworm (store), 60, 73, 74, 75, 77.
Boyd, Steve, 63, 109, 110, 111.
Brare, 65, 112, 138.
Brothers (organization), 74, 75.
Brown, Herman, 12.
Bulldog News, 132.

Burton, Philip, 87.

B

Cappers Flying Club, 95.
Carlson, Virginia, 16.
Carmichael, Stokely, 75.
Carpentier, Georges, 29.
Carrol, Charles O., 104.
Carroll, Major Ray, 122.
Central Area Motivation Program, 85.
Chamber of Commerce, 73, 74, 134, 135, 137.
Chambless, John, 77.
Chaney, Roy, 3.
Citizens Advisory Council, 126.
Clockwork Orange (band), 85, 86.
Code of Avenue Behavior, 79-80.
Communist Party, 87.
Community Council, 126, 137.
Condon, John, 31.
Conrad, Ernest, 62, 66, 93, 125, 138.
Coppage, Dick, 11, 97, 120.
Coppage, Tom, 113.
Corr, Assistant Police Chief, 120, 121.
Council of Churches, 135.
Crowley, George, 83-84.
Crowley, Walt, 59, 60, 64, 74, 78, 79, 80, 93-94, 109, 110-114, 126, 138.

D

The Daily (University of Washington), 78, 106.

De Haro Hotel, 44.
Delay, Jack and Sally, 59-60, 74.
Desmond, Jeff, 102, 103-105.
Devine, Ed (Seattle Deputy Mayor), 79.
Diamond (store), 31, 126.
Dixon, Elmer, 76.
Doolittle, Ed, 48.
Dorpat, Paul, 60, 61, 74, 138.
Douglas, Justice William O., 49.
Doukhabors, 87, 88.
Durant, Will, 14.
Dwyer, William L., 73.

E

Egyptian Theatre, 29.
Eigerwand Coffee House, 68.
Emerson, Jim, 96.
Encore Cafe, 67-68.

F

Falk, Officer Dennis, 80.
Fanchon & Marco Review, 29.
Flag Protection Act, 88.
Foster, Mike and Pam, 27-28.

G

the Gap (store), 31.
Garfield, Ted, 80.
Glasson, Gene and Dollie, 49.
Godfather's Pizza, 31.
Goodwin, U.S. District Court Judge William, 105.
Gough, George, 118.
Grand Opera House, 30.
Grant, Roxy, 113, 138.
Grasby, Sgt. Don, 80.
Grinnel McLean (store), 127.
Gunn, Thom, 63, 91, 93.

H

Hahn, Freeman, 11.
Haliburton, Richard, 14.
Hanson, Police Chief Robert, 104.

Harrington, Bill, 109, 110.
Hartman, Jack, 19.
Headley, "Barnacle Bill," 46.
Helen Rickert (store), 127.
The Helix, 59, 60, 61, 73, 79.
Herold, Steve, 73, 75, 77.
Hogness, John, 106.
Holloway, Doc, 30.
Housing Advisory Board, 48.

I

the Id (store), 73, 74, 75, 77.
International Socialist Organization (ISO), 135.
Iverson, Stan, 86-87.

J

Jackson, Terry Peter (aka Trim Bissel), 102.
Jenkins, Charley, 94.
Jessup, Dave, 122.
Johanson, Bruce, 78.
John Deere Co., 19.
Jones & Bronson, 36.

K

Kantz, O. E., 121.
Kennedy, Don, 128.
Kent State shootings, 4, 69-70, 98, 117.
Kinko's, 31.
Kirchoffer, John, 13.
Kirschner, Lee, 70.
Koch, Willis, 30.
Kress (store), 31, 127.
Ku Klux Klan, 7.
Kwakiutl tribe, 52-55.

L

Lacitis, Erik, 89, 105.
Lambert, X. A., 17.
La Tienda (store), 97, 132.
Lawrie, Walter J., 34-36.
Lawson, George, 65.

Leary, Timothy, 70, 75.
Leffel, Dick, 109, 110, 111, 138.
Lerners (store), 127.
the Limited (store), 31.

M

Mahoney, Police Chief Neal, 97, 98.
Maleng, Norm, 133.
Manolides, Judge, 85, 87.
Martin & Eckman (store), 127.
Matheson, Captain Mel, 80.
McCord, Bill, 126.
McCune, Calmar (grandfather), 8.
McCune, Calmar (father), 3, 9, 12, 14-21, 39, 138-139.
McCune, Cal Jr. "Mac" (son), 36, 39-40, 42, 47-48, 50-56.
McCune, Grace Montgomery (mother), 10, 14-15, 139.
McCune, Leslie (daughter), 33, 34, 39-40, 42, 47-48, 50, 51, 97.
McCune, Margaret (grandmother), 6-7, 9.
McCune, Peg (wife), 2-4, 29, 32-37, 39-41, 45, 47-48, 97, 113, 118, 119, 127, 132.
McCune, Wes (brother), 15, 16, 139.
McGovern, Judge Walter, 102.
McMillin, John S., 44-45.
McMillin, Paul, 45.
McNeil Island Penitentiary, 104.
Meakins, Buster, 16, 30, 138.
Meany Hotel, 28.
the Metropolitan (theatre), 30.
Miller, Carl, 107.
Miller, Acting Mayor Floyd, 97.
Milnes, Special (FBI) Agent J. Earl, 105.
Mitsulas, John, 61, 76, 91, 92, 96, 97, 98, 109, 110, 111, 120, 121, 138.
Mix, Tom, 16.

Monsoon (store), 132.
Moore, Police Chief, 120, 121, 122.
the Moore (theatre), 29.
Municipal League, 61.
Murphy, James "Murph," 29, 30.
Murphy, T. J., 28.

N

The Nation, 104.
National Recovery Act, 32.
New American Movement, 114.
Nielsen, Roy, 97.

O

Odegaard, Charles, 63, 107, 138.
O. Henry, 14.
Open Door Clinic, 70.
Owen, Henry B., 34-36.

P

Pacific National Bank, 98.
Pamir House (coffee house), 68.
Paramount (theatre), 29.
Patton, Robert, 121.
potlatch, 54-55.
Peabody, Eddie, 29.
Penny's (store), 70, 126.
Pentages, 29.
Penthouse Theatre, 28.
Pinkney, David H., 106.
Pitcher, Jack, 29.
Pitcher's (store), 132.
Pitkin, Stan, 103.
Porter & Jenson Jewelers, 95, 132.
Porter, Warren, 95-96.

R

Rader, Miriam, 64.
Radford, Junior, 139.
Radio Shack, 132.
Rainier Club, 60.
Ramon, Police Chief Frank, 86.
Reed, Leroy P., 121.
Reed, Michael Stephen, 102.

Reedy, Cal (cousin), 17, 18.
Revolutionary Communist Youth
    Brigade, 136.
Richardson Associates, 126.
RKO Orpheum Theatre, 29.
Roche Harbor Lime and Cement
    Co., 44.
Rotary Club, 14, 20, 30, 49, 62.
Rowlands, David D., 125, 128.
Royer, Dave, 64, 109, 110, 111.

S

Safeco Insurance Co., 125.
Scott, Louis C., 86.
Seattle Magazine, 84.
Seattle Planning Commission, 48,
    117.
Seattle *Post Intelligencer*, 105.
Seattle *Times*, 3, 78, 80, 89, 105.
Shaw, Robert Bernard, 67-68.
Shiga, Andy, 58-59, 61-62, 79, 91,
    92, 96, 109, 138.
Shiga's One World Shop, 132.
Shupe, Bob, 109, 110.
Sidran, Mark, 135.
Sidran Ordinance, 135, 136, 137.
Silverman, Rick, 63.
Smith, Judge Charles Z., 84-85.
Smith, Moncrieff H., 121, 122.
Smith, Sam, 97.
Smoke Shop (store), 94.
Stander, Tim, 120, 121.
Starbuck's, 132.
Stern, Robbie and Suzi, 59, 66, 74.
the Street Caucus, 78, 79.
Students for a Democratic Society
    (SDS), 64, 65, 66.
Sweeney, Gordon, 125.

T

Tissot, Jan, 61, 70-71, 78, 79, 80-
    81, 100-103.
Tower Records, 127.

Town Shop, 127.
TRA (architectural firm), 126.
Turner, Floyd, 83-89.

U

Uhlman, Mayor Wes, 123.
United Fruit Company, 66.
United States v. Eichman, 88.
Universal Life Church, 74.
University Book Store, 31, 32, 62,
    127.
University Congregational Church,
    114.
University District Center, 62, 64,
    109-115.
University District Development
    Council, 125.
University District Herald, 77.
University District Movement, 71,
    73-81.
University District Street Fair, 83.
University Street Caucus, 78, 79.
University Village, 133, 134.
University of Washington, 31, 126,
    128, 137.

V

VanLoon, Henrik, 14.
Van Veenendal, John Edward, 192.

W

Wagner, Bill, 47.
Ward, Larry, 103-104.
Weathermen, 64, 101.
Weiner, Steve, 106.
West, Monty, 70.
Westin Hotel, 29.
Weyerhauser, 65.
Whalen, Officer Robert, 80.
Whisler, Patty, 137.
Wierman, Louise, 110.
Wilson, John Wesley, 6-7, 9.
Wilson, James "Jim," 6-7, 9, 18, 20.

Wilson, Margaret McCune (aunt),
    6-7, 9.
Wilsonian Hotel, 28, 30.
Winebar, Sam, 15.
Wiseman, Burt, 26.
Wiseman's Cafe, 4, 24-28.
Wiseman, Dick, 25, 28, 32.
Wood, Edmund J., 85.
Woolworth's, 31, 126.
Worcester, Dean, 46, 50.
Worcester, Joy, 46.
Worcester, Mary, 50.
World's Fair (1962), 66.
Wyne, Mike, 78, 80.

Y

Yesler Atlantic Project, 48.
Younger, Willy, 68.